Cooking Gluten Free

Gerry Koprowski

Healthy Recipes for Everyone

© Copyright 2012 by Gerry Koprowski

ISBN 978-0-9831300-7-9

Illustrations by Gerry Koprowski

Cover by Laura Driscoll.

Third Printing October, 2013

All rights reserved. No part of this book may be reproduced or transmitted in any form without written permission of the publisher, except by reviewers who may quote brief excerpts in connection with a review.

Windjammer Adventure Publishing
289 South Franklin Street, Chagrin Falls, OH 44022
Telephone 440.247.6610 Email windjammerpub@mac.com

Recipes for a Gluten Free Life

When my husband, Ken and granddaughter Daisy, were both diagnosed with Celiac disease I bought every cookbook for gluten free recipes on the shelves. I poured over library books and sniffed out any article on the illness that was available. I spent hours on the internet researching recipes and listing every gluten item I could find. I did learn a lot!

After bringing home bread from the store that could be used as a weapon and putting out cakes that crumbled into small mounds I just knew I could somehow do better. They deserved better!

The long project of baking, making and tasting began. I wanted to make food that had little or no additives or chemicals. I knew that many gluten free items are loaded with additives, fructose, words I could not pronounce, tons of salt and a large amount of sugar. People who cook for Celiacs know the basics once they get the diagnoses. The trick is to get things to taste good and also to be healthy for everyone. Back to basics and to simple food. We all know meat, fish, fresh vegetables and fruit are the safest foods to eat, as they are naturally gluten free. What about a good onion ring or tasty donut? Could we again have an additive free pudding or lemonade? Should we think that a cinnamon roll is out of reach? Do our eyes light up with a thin crusted Italian pizza? Again, simple, easy to make but also passing the thumbs up test from my darling Daisy! So this book came to be. These are the best for the best!

Afterward

The next step after providing you with great recipes for you to cook is to also offer you other items for your freezer. Again, our products will be made with ingredients free of gluten, chemicals and additives. The products will be produced under the name of Two Flowers Food Company. Time, effort and love will be baked into our Two Flowers line.

This book is produced for my granddaughters, the original "Two Flowers", London Rose and Daisy Elizabeth Koprowski. The third flower who has helped me so much has been named "Lilly" even though her name is Kara Spidle, my daughter. Daisy felt this would be a perfect name for her! Love to all three and to everyone who cheered me on! Gerry Koprowski, GeeGee

Brief Bio

In 1979 I opened a small tearoom named "Trifles". I have been cooking and working with food ever since. The tearoom and four locations later eventually evolved into Trifles Cafe and Catering. This catering division is still going strong today! I know food and I love it!

Table of Contents

Appetizers, Beverages & Dips ◆ 1

Bread Products, Pancakes & Crusts ◆ 17

Make Your Own Mixes & Pantry Staples ◆ 37

Satisfying Meals ◆ 47

Sauces & Dressings ◆ 77

Soups & Salads ◆ 97

Sweet Tooth ◆ 129

Vegetables & Sides ◆ 165

Index ◆ 182i

Stocking a Gluten-Free Pantry 101

- Vegan substitutes can be used for most recipes unless noted
- Eggs, I use large
- Unsalted butter
- Milk: Regular whole milk, buttermilk, half and half, heavy cream. Most recipes do not work well with nonfat milk.
- Sour cream
- Yogurt, any kind, any fat content unless noted. No "lite" or artificially flavored.
- Dry buttermilk powder
- Non-fat dry milk powder
- Potato starch or potato starch flour, they are the same thing
- Potato flour, tapioca flour, Rice flour-white, brown and sweet
- Xanthan gum
- Sorghum flour
- Almond flour and other nut flours
- All Purpose GF Flour or see Two Flowers recipe for homemade
- Quinoa and quinoa flour
- Buckwheat flour, there is no wheat in buckwheat
- Yeast, dry in packets
- Cornstarch
- Baking powder, see Two Flowers recipe to avoid having aluminum in your food
- Cornmeal
- Breading and coatings, see Two Flowers recipes
- Rice and corn pasta, see Two Flowers recipe for homemade
- Nuts: Raw or plain roasted
- Honey: Agave nectar or pure maple syrup
- Sugar: White, brown sugar light and dark, raw, powdered sugar, and coconut syrup
- Oil: Including olive, corn, vegetable, peanut, coconut, rice and canola
- GF Cooking spray: Vegetable and olive oil make sure it is additive free
- GF Soy sauce: Tamari style soy sauce, La Choy, even though it is not labeled GF
- Vinegar: Many options are white, balsamic, rice, champagne, red wine, and cider not malt
- Worcestershire sauce: Lea and Perrins
- Mayonnaise: Hellman's, also see Two Flowers recipe for homemade
- Catsup/Ketchup: Heinz, also see Two Flowers recipe for homemade
- Mustard: Guldens, Grey Poupon, and Heinz
- Table salt: Sea salt fine and coarse but in my recipes I am referring to coarse sea salt
- Pepper: Fresh ground from black peppercorns
- Fresh ginger root
- Spices are so necessary to turn items from "bland" to "wow"
- Pure vanilla extract
- Pure almond extract

Tips From Gee Gee's Kitchen - Simple Clean Food

- Do not buy farm grown fish. Pay more for wild, ocean, or lake fish.
- Buy grass fed beef. It is clean and hormone free. Processed meats may have hidden gluten in them. Check all your chicken, pork and lamb products.
- Stay away from MSG.
- Some processed food is loaded with salt, sugar, chemicals, and dyes of allkind. These additives prolong shelf life and add flavor to tasteless GF products.
- Try to make fresh whenever you can and eat as you go.
- Unsalted butter is a good choice for cooking. It does not burn as quickly as salted butter.
- Peanut oil has a higher burning point than regular canola oil.
- Change your frying oil if you fry wheat items. Never try to reuse.
- Cook rice in GF broth instead of water. It flavors it.
- Glass jars with lids are great for storing GF flours and mixes. Plastic can absorb food and germs. Glass can be safely washed at high temperatures in your dishwasher.
- GF baked goods burn quicker and dry out faster. Always cover them. Freeze or refrigerate when possible.
- Use light, bright baking sheets and not dark coated ones. Baked goods burn faster on dark surfaces. Invest in new baking pans and sheets. Buy the sizes you use the most for your family size. The pizza pans with perforations in the bottom will give you a better crust. If you are sharing a kitchen with "wheat folks" keep your kitchen utensils and pans separate. Buy a new toaster, rolling pin and flour sifter. Invest in silicone spatulas and toss the rubber ones out!
- Try to go stainless with everything. I do not use coated pots and pans or coated utensils.
- Use new cutting boards. Years of gluten build up can be on your old ones.
- If cooking in a glass pan, reduce your heat by 25 degrees.

- To clean fruit and vegetables, wash with a few teaspoons of bleach in the water. There are also over the counter products that do a good job.
- Refrigerate all fruit and even tomatoes. Times have changed and bacteria lives on these items. Celiac patients have enough problems without adding more stomach upsets.
- Use only pasteurized eggs for any uncooked product you are making such as mousse or any unbaked product.
- Xanthan gum is necessary to "glue" the flours together. When in doubt use at least a pinch.
- If your baked goods turn out too dry, add moisture like fruit juice, applesauce, yogurt, mayonnaise, or sour cream when you make the recipe again.
- Keep trying recipes out. Don't give up on the first try. You may need to modify with more sugar, salt, etc. to meet your own taste.
- Cross contamination is huge. The pesky wheat crumbs and flour are everywhere. In your kitchen, label, label, label!
- A doughnut machine will give you lovely doughnuts without frying.
- Learn to whisk GF flours instead of beating them. They are more fragile.
- I like to cook with cream but you can substitute any milk or non-dairy milk in recipes.
- Seasonings are so important in GF cooking. In many commercially prepared items, high sodium and hidden gluten can be found. The word "blend" may have hidden gluten. Bottom line is seasonings may or may not be gluten free. Easy to make your own seasonings from a Two Flowers recipe.

Hidden Gluten Foods

Read labels carefully. Anything processed, bottled, boxed or packaged may have gluten! Here are some common items that have gluten in them:

- Pre-marinated meats and fish
- Seasoning packages in prepared foods or boxes
- Bouillon cubes, broths and granular bouillon, except Herb Ox
- Candy may have a coating of flour such as licorice, malt chocolate, hard candies
- Canned and frozen soup
- Frozen entrees
- Processed cheese
- Chinese condiments
- Cold cuts and processed meats
- Dip mixes
- Dry roasted nuts and honey nuts
- Gravies
- Rice syrup and brown rice syrup may contain gluten, don't let the word "rice" fool you.
- Dry sauces
- Spices and spice mixes may have wheat added to prevent clumping
- Liquid smoke seasoning or smoked anything!
- Herb teas may contain gluten. In many cases Decaf coffee may be processed with wheat. Drink only regular coffee. Instant or flavored coffee may contain gluten.
- Beer and liquor
- Seasoned raw meat may have fillers
- Sausage mixes
- Communion wafers
- Imitation seafood or coated, seasoned fish filets
- Bottled dressings and sauces
- Non-dairy creamers
- Some ice cream and frozen treats
- Toothpaste
- Lip balm, lipstick
- Soap, shampoo, lotion
- Stamps, back of envelopes

- Vitamins and over-the-counter medicines
- Vegetable Gum
- Vegetable protein
- MSG
- Extenders
- Binders
- Dextrin
- Maltose
- Artificial flavors
- Natural colors
- Pet food (wear gloves when touching it)
- Play dough (recipe for gluten free play dough is as follows:)

1 C. white rice flour
½ C. cornstarch
½ C. table salt
1 Tbs. cream of tartar
1 C. hot water (not boiling)
1 ½ tsp. oil (not olive)
GF food coloring, liquid

Mix dry ingredients, add oil and water. Mix together in a saucepan over medium heat, stirring for about 3 minutes. The dough will form a ball. Turn the dough ball out on to a piece of wax or parchment paper. Cool. Make a small hole in the center of the ball and put a drop of food coloring into the hole. Knead the food coloring into the dough ball. You can add more for darker colors. Store the balls in plastic bags or jars.

- Hairspray
- Kingsford Charcoal

Just remember manufacturers regularly change their ingredients, always read the label.

What I Learned from Eating in Restaurants

While nothing is better than preparing your food at home, there are gluten-free fast food restaurant items. A fast food item may be good in a pinch but again, be ever vigilant! You must be careful of cross contamination. Check to make sure grills do not have bread on them and that they do not fry things in oil used for gluten products. Some fast food restaurants that have gluten-free options but there is no guarantee any fast food item will be truly gluten-free. Some restaurants have better options than others such as a Wendy's salad and baked potato but you have to be careful to not use the packets of nuts in the salad. Some of the best options are found at Chipotle Grill. All beef is hormone free and they have many gluten-free options including corn tortillas, toppings and greens. Chick-fil-a has many choices including fries.

The Following Chains Have Extensive Gluten-Free Menu Choices:
T.G.I Fridays, P.F. Chang's, Outback Steakhouse, Bonefish Grill, Ruby Tuesday, Applebee's, Olive Garden, and Panera.

Guidelines to Follow for Independent Restaurants

Again and foremost, look out for cross contamination. Question everything. When in doubt DO NOT EAT! Most non-chain restaurants are more knowledgeable about food issues and the food that they are cooking. Make sure the part of the grill that your food will be cooked on is cleaned and pans washed first. I know it is a little extra trouble but it is worth it. Have your salad made in a clean bowl. Use only vinegar and oil or carry your own dressing. In an ice cream store, make sure the scoop is washed before your ice cream is scooped. Request that your food be kept away from the bread basket. Do not be afraid to discuss all your needs with your server. Restaurant dining cards can be printed from **glutenfreerestaurants.org** and **Celiactravel.com** that you can give to a waiter if you are eating in a restaurant. It will list what to avoid in their cooking practices. That way you don't have to grill the waiter.

Happy, Healthy Eating!

Appetizers, Beverages & Dips

Asparagus Fries

3 C. canola oil
2 eggs, beaten
1 medium lime, juiced
3/4 C. GF all purpose flour, see Two Flowers recipe
1/4 tsp. sea salt
1/8 tsp. pepper
1 C. rice crackers, crushed
1 lb. thick cut asparagus

Dipping Sauce:
4 garlic cloves, peeled, crushed
2/3 C. GF mayonnaise, see Two Flowers recipe
1 T. olive oil
1 tsp. paprika
1 tsp. fresh lemon juice
1/4 tsp. sea salt
1/8 tsp. pepper

Preheat oven to 200°. Whisk eggs with lime juice and 2 tablespoons of water. Put flour in a small bowl with salt and pepper. In another bowl put the crushed rice crackers. Dredge the asparagus in flour. Dip the asparagus in eggs, coating completely and then coat with rice crumbs. Fry the asparagus about 3 minutes and drain on paper towels. Keep warm in a 200° oven. Yield: about 20
Dipping sauce: Mix all dipping sauce ingredients together and refrigerate.

Bacon, Lettuce and Tomato Fritters

1/2 lb. cooked GF bacon, chopped
3/4 C. GF baking mix, see Two Flowers recipe
1/2 C. crumbled GF Rice Chex
1 C. tomatoes, chopped, drained
2 tsp. fresh garlic, minced
2 tsp. red wine vinegar
2 tsp. sugar

1 tsp. fresh basil, chopped
1 tsp. sea salt
1/4 tsp. black pepper
GF Mayonnaise, see Two Flowers recipe
Iceberg, romaine or butter lettuce cups
Canola oil for frying

Preheat oven to 200°. Combine all ingredients except baking mix and GF Rice Chex. Stir in the baking mix and crumbled GF Rice Chex into the combined ingredients. By the tablespoon, drop the batter into hot oil and fry fritters until brown, about 3 minutes. Oil should be at 350°. Keep warm in a 200° oven as you fry the rest of the fritters. Serve in a small lettuce cup. The ones listed in the ingredient list work the best. Top with a dollop of mayonnaise. Yield: 12 fritters

Baked Tortilla Chips

12 corn tortillas, white or yellow
1/2 tsp. granulated garlic
1/4 C. Parmesan cheese, grated
2 T. Italian seasoning, see Two Flowers recipe
GF cooking spray
1/2 tsp. sea salt

Preheat oven to 375°. Cut tortillas into wedges and spray with cooking spray. Mix seasonings, except the salt, and sprinkle on the wedges. Line a baking sheet with foil and bake the wedges at 375° until crisp. The time will vary as to the thickness of the tortillas. When they are crisp, sprinkle on the sea salt. Cool.

Beet Hummus

2 C. dried cannellini white beans, cooked
1 C. fresh beets, cooked
1/4 C. tahini
2 T. fresh lemon juice
1 T. fresh horseradish
2 garlic cloves, minced
1 tsp. salt
1/4 C. olive oil
1/8 C. parsley, chopped

See Two Flowers recipe for cooking dried beans. See below for how to roast beets. Combine cooked beans, cooked beets, tahini, lemon juice, horseradish, garlic and salt in a food processor. Blend until smooth. Add oil to the running processor through the feeding tube. Transfer to a serving bowl. Top with chopped parsley. Use your favorite GF chips or vegetables as scoops. Yield: 3 cups

Note: To roast beets, wash thoroughly. Leave skins on but remove greens. Toss with olive oil. Bake covered in a baking dish at 350° for 45-60 minutes until a knife slides easily through the largest beet. When cool, the skins will slide off.

Blue Cheese Cheesecake

16 oz. cream cheese, softened
16 oz. blue cheese, crumbled
1 1/4 C. sour cream
3 eggs, beaten
2 T. GF all purpose flour, see Two Flowers recipe
1/2 tsp. salt
1/3 tsp. white pepper
1 tsp. sugar
Garnish:
2 T. fresh chives, chopped
2 T. fresh parsley, chopped
1/2 C. pecans, chopped

Preheat oven to 300°. Beat cream cheese and blue cheese together. Add 1 cup of the sour cream and sugar along with the GF flour to the mix. Add eggs one at a time. Add seasonings. Pour batter into a buttered 9 inch springform pan. Wrap foil around the pan to keep the filling from oozing out. Bake in a 300° oven for 1 hour. Test the center with a toothpick to see if it comes out clean. Spread the reserved 1/4 cup of sour cream over the top of the cheesecake. Bake for 5 minutes more. Remove from oven. Cool. Loosen from the edges and put on a serving plate. Top with the pecans, chopped chives and parsley. Cool about 30 minutes before serving. Great with fruit slices instead of crackers.

Cheese Straws

4 oz. sharp cheddar cheese, shredded
1/4 C. unsalted butter
1/2 C. cornstarch
1/3 C. potato starch
1/4 C. xanthan gum
1/4 tsp. red pepper flakes, optional
3 T. cream
Pinch of salt
1/4 C. Parmesan cheese, grated for topping

Preheat oven to 375°. Set aside the Parmesan cheese. Combine all the dry ingredients in a food processor or a mixer. Add the cream. This dough will be crumbly. Pat it out on the counter into a 1/4 inch thickness. Proceed to cut the dough into appetizer-sized strips. Sprinkle with Parmesan cheee. If you find that the dough is too sticky, put it into the refrigerator for 20 minutes and try again. Place the straws on a greased, parchment paper lined cookie sheet and bake for 12 minutes. Cool.

Cheesy Rice Balls

1 1/4 C. Arborio or risotto rice, cooked
12 to 15 small chunks of fresh mozzarella cheese
1 egg, beaten
1/2 C. crushed GF rice crackers
1/4 tsp. sea salt
1/8 tsp. pepper
2 T. parsley, minced
Olive oil for frying

Cook rice according to the package directions. Refrigerate the rice. Mix seasoning and parsley with cold rice. Roll the cold rice into an appetizer sized ball. Put a small mozzarella cube into the center of each ball. Make sure you work the rice around the cube. Roll each ball into the beaten egg then roll it into the cracker mixture to coat. Heat olive oil in a skillet and brown the rice ball until golden. Serve hot. Yield: 12 to 15 appetizers

Chex Mix Munchies

7 C. GF Chex cereal
1 C. mixed nuts
1 C. GF pretzels
2 C. air popped popcorn, see Two Flowers recipe for microwave popcorn
6 T. unsalted butter
2 T. Worcestershire sauce
1 1/2 tsp. sea salt
3/4 tsp. garlic powder
1/2 tsp. onion powder
1/4 C. Parmesan cheese, grated

In a 200° oven, melt butter in a roasting pan. Stir in seasonings. Use unseasoned GF chex cereal. Toss to coat all the dry ingredients. Bake for 1 hour, mixing occasionally to distribute the butter and seasoning. Cool for 15 minutes on a paper towel. Store tightly covered. Yield: Approximately 11 to 12 cups.

Chicken Nuggets
No need to fry

1 1/2 lbs. boneless, skinless chicken breasts
2 eggs, beaten
1/2 C. GF all purpose flour, see Two Flowers recipe

2 C. crushed GF Chex or GF Corn Flakes cereal
1/2 C. Parmesan cheese, grated
2 T. powdered sugar
3 T. unsalted butter, melted

Preheat oven to 400°. Cut the chicken breasts into 2 x 2 inch cubes. Prepare 3 bowls with breading ingredients. Mix Parmesan with your coating choice for one bowl. Put beaten eggs in another bowl. Mix the GF flour with the sugar and put it into a 3rd. bowl. Dip the chicken into the flour then into the beaten eggs. Finally roll the chicken in the coating of choice and put the coated cubes on a sheet pan lined parchment paper. Drizzle nuggets with melted butter. Bake uncovered for 10 to 12 minutes. Yield: 6 servings.

Chili Con Queso Dip

3 T. olive oil
1 C. green onions, bulbs and tops, minced
3 fresh jalapeno peppers, seeded and minced
1 red bell pepper, seeded and minced
2 C. plum tomatoes, diced
2 C. light cream

6 oz. cream cheese
8 oz. Jack cheese, shredded
8 oz. sharp cheddar cheese, shredded
2 T. GF all purpose flour, see Two Flowers recipe
1 T. cumin
1/4 tsp. sea salt
1/8 tsp. pepper

Heat oil and sauté the green onions and both peppers until they are softened. DO NOT BOIL. Remove from the heat. Cut the cream cheese into small pieces and add it to the sauce. Stir until melted. Add the light cream. Toss the 2 cheeses with the flour to coat them. Add the cheese to the sauce a little at a time and stir. Should be mostly melted. Return to heat. Add seasonings and tomatoes. Serve warm with your choice of dippers. Yield: about 4 cups

Chili Cheese Squares

4 T. unsalted butter, melted
5 large eggs
1/4 C. GF baking flour mix, see Two Flowers recipe
1/2 tsp. baking powder, see Two Flowers recipe

1 4 oz. jar mild green chilies
1/2 C. small curd cottage cheese
2 C. pepper cheese, shredded

Preheat oven to 400°. To beaten eggs, stir in flour and baking powder. Add butter and stir in remaining ingredients. Pour into a greased 9 x 9 inch square pan. Bake at 400° for 15 minutes. Reduce heat to 350°. Bake for 30 minutes more. Cool slightly and cut into appetizer-size squares. Yield: will depend upon the cut size. I like a 2 inch x 2 inch size.

Coconut Chicken Fingers
A different twist for chicken fingers

1 1/2 lbs. chicken breast
1/2 tsp. salt
1/4 tsp. cayenne pepper
1 C. rice flour

1 C. buttermilk
1 egg, beaten
1 1/2 C. unsweetened coconut
3 T. canola oil

Cut chicken breasts into 1/2 inch strips. Sprinkle chicken with seasonings. Put flour into one dish and buttermilk mixed with egg in another dish. A third dish will hold coconut. Dredge chicken in flour, then egg, then coconut. Add oil to pan and cook strips for about 6 minutes until done. Brown on all sides. Yield: 6 4 ounce servings

Crab Cakes

- 1 lb. lump crab meat
- 2 eggs, beaten
- 4 T. potato starch
- 1/4 C. GF mayonnaise, see Two Flowers recipe
- 1/4 C. sweet onion, finely chopped
- 1/4 C. celery, finely chopped
- 2 T. parsley, finely chopped
- 1 tsp. Worcestershire sauce
- 1 tsp. Old Bay seasoning
- 1 tsp. fresh lemon juice
- 1 tsp. dry mustard
- 1 tsp. sea salt
- Canola oil for frying
- Tartar sauce - see Two Flowers recipe

Try Phillips pure crab meat in the can if you are not using frozen or fresh crab meat. Incorporate all ingredients except oil until thoroughly mixed. Cover and chill for 30 minutes. Divide into 1/4 cup servings for each cake. Form the mixture with your hands into small cakes. Put each cake into hot oil for frying. Use a large pan and cook over medium heat. Cook 5 minutes until brown. Turn over and cook an additional 4 to 5 minutes on the other side. Yield: 16 appetizer-sized cakes. Serve with tartar sauce on the side.

Crunchy Chicken Fingers
Everyone loves chicken fingers

- 1 1/2 lbs. chicken breasts
- 1/2 C. GF mayonnaise, see Two Flowers recipe
- 1 tsp. paprika
- 1 C. GF potato chips, crushed

Preheat oven to 400°. Cut chicken breasts into 1 inch strips. Do not salt them. Coat them with GF mayonnaise mixed with paprika. In the food processor pulse the chips to a coarse texture. Remove the chips to a flat surface. Roll strips carefully in the processed chips. Bake strips on a parchment lined cookie sheet at 400° for 10 to 12 minutes. Yield: 6 4 ounce servings

Hummus
Restaurant Style

1 T. lemon juice
1/4 C. water
6 T. tahini
2 T. olive oil
1 1/2 C. chick peas, cooked
1 garlic clove, minced

1/2 tsp. salt
1/4 tsp. cumin
Sprinkle of cayenne
1 T. cilantro, minced
1 T. parsley, minced
Green onion, tops and bulbs, thinly sliced

See Two Flowers recipe for cooking dried beans. In a small bowl, combine lemon juice and water. Whisk together tahini and olive oil. Process cooked chickpeas, garlic, salt, cumin and cayenne. Keep the processor running and add lemon juice/water mixture. Process until the hummus is creamy and smooth. Sprinkle the cilantro and parsley over the top with the green onion slices and drizzle with additional olive oil. Yield: 2 cups

Kale Chips
Kara Koprowski   Oven baked

1 medium sized bunch of kale
1/2 T. apple cider vinegar
2 T. olive oil

3 T. Parmesan cheese, grated
1 tsp. coarse sea salt

Heat oven to 375°. Wash and dry kale. Fold each kale leaf in half and remove the stem with a sharp knife. Tear kale into 3 to 4 inch pieces and place in a large bowl. In a small bowl, mix vinegar and oil. Pour over kale in bowl and toss well. Place kale in a single layer on a large baking sheet and sprinkle with salt and cheese. Bake 10 to 15 minutes until kale is crispy. Will be slightly brown around the edges. Store in a paper bag for 1 to 2 days.

Microwave Popcorn
Easy, chemical free alternative to the box

1/2 C. popping corn	Chili powder
1 tsp. canola oil	Onion
1/2 tsp. salt	Garlic salt
Brown lunch bags	Cinnamon
Additions:	Sugar
Parmesan cheese	Butter and salt are a classic combination

In a bowl mix the popcorn and oil. If you want the salt to stick on the popcorn pulse it to a really fine grind. Sprinkle on the salt. Seal the bag by folding it over twice. Microwave on high for 2 1/2 minutes to 3 minutes with the bag standing up and not on its side. Do not paper clip or staple the bag.

Mini Corn Dogs
Kids and adults love this appetizer.

Vegetable oil for frying	1 tsp. sea salt
1/4 C. cornstarch	1/2 C. additional GF all purpose flour
1 lb. GF beef hot dogs	3 T. sugar
1 1/2 C. cornmeal	1 1/4 C. buttermilk
6 T. GF all purpose flour, see Two Flowers recipe	40 6" skewers soaked in water
2 T. baking powder, see Two Flowers recipe	

Heat a dutch oven with 4 inches of oil on top the stove to 350°. Cut the hot dogs into 4 pieces. Put each piece on it's own skewer. Soaking the skewers will prevent them from burning. Combine cornmeal, 6 tablespoons of flour, baking powder, and sea salt in a bowl. Add the additional flour and sugar to the cornmeal mix. Add buttermilk and whisk until a smooth batter is formed. Put cornstarch in a bowl and dip each hot dog piece into corn starch, tapping off the excess. Dip the hot dog into the batter covering the whole piece. Fry until brown and drain on paper towels. Yield: 40 appetizer pieces.

Norwegian Salmon Spread

8 oz. cream cheese
1/2 C. sour cream
1 T. fresh lemon juice
1 T. fresh dill
1 tsp. pure horseradish

1/2 tsp. sea salt
1/4 tsp. pepper
6 oz. smoked Norwegian salmon, minced

With a mixer whip the cream cheese. Add the sour cream to make a spread. Add the rest of the seasonings. Stir in the salmon. Refrigerate until serving. Use with GF crackers or GF bread. This spread can also be used with fresh vegetables.
Yield: 2 cups

Seared Fingerling Potatoes with Gorgonzola Cream Dip

Kara Koprowski

Seared Potatoes:
1 1/2 lbs. yellow fingerling potatoes
1 tsp. olive oil
1 shallot, chopped
2 garlic cloves, minced
1 tsp. salt
1 tsp. pepper
Gorgonzola Cream Dip:
1 C. sour cream

1/2 C. heavy cream
8 oz. cream cheese, room temperature
1 tsp. lemon zest
1 T. fresh lemon juice
2 garlic cloves, minced
1 C. Gorgonzola cheese, crumbled (can substitute another blue cheese if desired)

Scrub potatoes but do not peel. Place potatoes in large saucepan with salted water to cover. Bring to a boil, reduce heat and cover. Simmer until tender about 10 to 15 minutes. Drain. Test tenderness with a knife. Smaller potatoes may cook faster. Pat dry and cut potatoes in half lengthwise and set aside. In a large skillet over medium heat sauté oil, shallots and garlic until light brown, about 5 minutes. Add potatoes and sauté until golden brown. Add salt and pepper. In a food processor pulse sour cream, heavy cream and cream cheese until well combined and smooth. Add lemon zest, juice, garlic, salt and pepper to taste. Empty mixture into a bowl and add blue cheese. Serve with warm potatoes.

Spinach and Artichoke Dip

- 14 oz. can of non-marinated artichoke hearts, chopped and drained
- 1 C. frozen spinach
- 8 oz. cream cheese
- 1/2 C. GF mayonnaise, see Two Flowers recipe
- 1/2 C. Parmesan cheese, grated
- 1/4 C. Romano cheese, grated
- 1 garlic clove, minced
- 1 tsp. fresh basil, slivered
- 1 tsp. fresh lemon juice
- 1/4 tsp sea salt

Optional:
- 1/2 lb. shrimp, frozen or fresh, shelled and deveined
- 1 T. unsalted butter, melted

Preheat oven to 350°. Cook shrimp in 1 T. butter until pink but still firm. Set aside. Thaw and squeeze-dry spinach. In a saucepan over medium heat, mix all ingredients except 1/4 cup Parmesan cheese and shrimp. When mixture is warm scoop into a buttered casserole dish. Bake at 350° for 30 minutes, uncovered. If you are using shrimp add on top of dip now. Garnish with reserved Parmesan cheese.

Spring Rolls

- 2 T. canola oil
- 1/2 C. green onions, bulbs and tops, sliced
- 2 garlic cloves, minced
- 1 C. carrots, grated
- 1 tsp. fresh ginger, grated
- 3 C. red and green cabbage, mixed
- 2 C. shitake mushrooms, slivered or mushrooms of choice
- 1 tsp. sesame oil
- 1 tsp. sugar
- 2 T. GF soy sauce
- 1 T. rice vinegar
- 1/2 tsp. coarse sea salt
- 1/2 lb. pork, cut into small strips
- 1/2 lb. raw shrimp, cut into small pieces
- 12 rice wrappers

Dipping sauce:
- 1/4 C. GF soy sauce
- 1/4 C. rice vinegar
- 1/4 C. brown sugar
- 2 tsp. fresh ginger, grated
- 1 small hot pepper, diced

In the oil, sauté the carrots, cabbage, garlic, onions, pork and ginger. Add the shrimp and continue to sauté until shrimp is cooked. This will only take a few minutes. Shrimp will be pink but firm. Add mushrooms and cook them down. Add all seasonings and mix well. Make the filling a little crispy rather than totally limp. Divide the filling into 12 portions. Soak the rice wrapper in warm water for a few minutes. Fill the wrapper by placing the filling on the wrapper side that is closest to you. Roll it up tucking the sides in as you go along. Serve with dipping sauce. Yield: 12 rolls

Sweet Potato Chips

- 1/2 lb. sweet potatoes, not yams
- 2 T. olive oil
- 1/4 tsp. sea salt

Preheat oven to 400°. Scrub sweet potatoes but leave the skin on. Slice into very, very thin slices using a mandolin slicer or a very sharp knife. Arrange chips on a cookie sheet in a single layer. Drizzle with olive oil and bake at 400° for 15 minutes. It will take longer if the slices are thicker. Sprinkle with sea salt. These are also good sprinkled with garlic salt in place of sea salt.

3 Cheese Fondue

1 T. unsalted butter
1/2 C. sweet onion, minced
1 garlic clove, minced
3 C. Emmentaler cheese, shredded
2 C. sharp white cheddar cheese, shredded
1 C. Swiss or Gruyere cheese, shredded
2 T. cornstarch
1 tsp. dry mustard
1/4 tsp. nutmeg
12 oz. white wine
3 T. sherry or Kirsch
Assorted dippers:
Steamed vegetables
Potato slices
French fries
Apples
Pears

Melt butter in a saucepan. If your fondue pot can be put safely on the stove you can use the fondue pot as your saucepan. In the saucepan soften the onion and garlic clove until they start to caramelize. In another bowl toss the shredded cheeses with cornstarch, mustard and nutmeg. Add wine to the saucepan and add the tossed cheese, a little at a time, stirring all the time. When all the cheese is melted, add sherry and transfer to the fondue pot, if you are not already using the fondue pot for a saucepan. Yield: 5 cups

White Bean Dip

1 C. white beans, cooked
4 C. water
1 tsp. salt
1 1/2 T. cold water
1 1/2 T. lemon juice
1 1/2 T. olive oil
1 T. granulated garlic
1 T. coarse sea salt

See Two Flowers recipe for cooking dried beans. Put cooked beans into the food processor and puree. Add the remaining ingredients and continue to process until smooth. Yield: 1 cup

Zucchini Fritters

2 C. zucchini, grated
4 T. olive oil
1 1/2 tsp. sea salt
1/2 C. fresh parsley, minced
2 garlic cloves, minced
2 shallots, minced
1 tsp. fresh oregano

1/4 C. fresh dill, minced
2 eggs, beaten
1/2 C. Parmesan cheese, grated
1/3 C. GF all purpose flour. see Two Flowers recipe
2 T. fresh chives, minced

Let the zucchini drain down for a few minutes before using. Sauté the grated zucchini in 2 tablespoons of olive oil. Add salt to draw the moisture out. Sauté the zucchini until the water is totally evaporated. Squeeze the zucchini dry. Toss with all the dry ingredients. Add the beaten eggs to dry mixture. Use 2 tablespoons of mixture to form a small sized flat pancake. Fry for about 2 minutes on each side. Drain and salt again to taste. Yield: 12 appetizer- sized pancakes

Banana Almond Smoothie

Kara Koprowski - this is a great on- the- go breakfast that is not too sweet

1 C. unsweetened almond milk
1 large ripe banana, peeled, sliced and frozen
1 C. frozen blueberries
1 T. packed light brown sugar or 1 T. honey

1 tsp. GF pure vanilla
Sprinkle of ground nutmeg or cinnamon
Optional:
1 T. ground flax seeds or chia seeds added to mixture before blending

Any milk can be substituted for almond milk. Blueberries work the best but you can use any frozen berries. Blend ingredients in blender until smooth. Sprinkle nutmeg or cinnamon on top. Yield 2 servings.

Citrus and Ginger Beer Cooler
Kara Koprowski

4 to 5 lemons, depending on size
2 navel orange
1 C. fresh ginger, chopped
1 C. honey
1/2 C. sugar
1 1/2 C. orange juice
4 C. club soda, chilled

Finely grate skin from lemons and oranges to get 2 tablespoons of zest of each. Use the colored part of skin only and not the white pith. Squeeze juice from lemons to get 1/3 cup of juice. Reserve extra whole lemon and orange. Scrub and roughly chop ginger. Keep the skin on the ginger. In a food processor, pulse chopped ginger, honey and sugar until combined. Add fresh squeezed lemon and orange juices and process. Transfer to a lidded container. Add lemon and orange zest and 2 cups of boiling water. Stir until sugar dissolves. Cool to room temperature. Cover and refrigerate for at least 24 hours and up to 5 days. Using a mesh strainer, strain the ginger and juice base into a pitcher. Add thinly sliced orange and lemon circles and club soda. Serve over ice. Add fresh mint if desired. Yield: 8 to 10 servings

Energy Juice Drink
Kara Koprowski

This is a low glycemic index juice. Almonds and cinnamon help prevent blood sugar spikes.
1/2 C. blackberries
1/2 C. blueberries
1 pear
1 carrot
1/2 cucumber
1 small handful fresh spinach
1 piece fresh ginger, skin removed, about 1 tsp.
12 to 15 whole almonds
1/2 to 1 tsp. cinnamon

Use organic, washed and unwaxed produce whenever possible. Pears will add more sweetness if they are ripe. Soak almonds in water overnight. Drain the almonds before juicing. Stir in a sprinkle cinnamon after everything is juiced. This recipe is for use with a juicer or juice extractor. Yield: 1 8 ounce serving

Greenish Smoothie

1 C. fresh spinach, stems removed
1/2 C. milk of choice or coconut water
1 C. plain Greek yogurt
1/2 C. frozen berries
1 banana, peeled and frozen
1 tsp. honey
Pinch of cinnamon

In a blender, process spinach with milk or coconut water. Add yogurt and frozen fruit. Blend using medium speed until smooth. Can add 1/2 teaspoon GF pure vanilla. Yield: 1 serving

White Hot Chocolate

1/2 C. white chocolate chips
1 tsp. GF pure vanilla
3 C. whole milk
Whipped cream

In a saucepan, heat the milk until it forms bubbles. Add the white chocolate chips and whisk until melted. Stir in vanilla. Top with whipped cream. Yield: 3 cups

Bread Products, Pancakes & Crusts

Almond Flour Thin Crust Pizza
Slightly sweet crust

1 1/2 C. almond flour	1/4 tsp. baking soda
2 tsp. xanthan gum	1 large egg, room temperature
1/4 tsp. salt	1 T. olive oil + 1/4 tsp. oil for bottom of pan

Preheat oven to 350°. Mix dry ingredients in one bowl. Whisk egg and olive oil in second bowl and stir into dry ingredients. Make a dough. Press dough, with your fingers into a 12 inch pizza pan that has been lightly rubbed with 1/4 teaspoon olive oil. Build up a small edge with the dough so that it will hold fillings. Bake for 8 minutes at 350°. Top with your favorite items and bake 18 minutes longer on middle rack. Yield: 1 crust

Apple Almond Muffins

1 1/2 C. apples, peeled and chopped	3/4 C. almonds, slivered
1 T. lemon juice	3/4 C. sugar
2 tsp. sugar	2 eggs
2 C. GF all purpose flour mix or GF pancake mix, see Two Flowers recipes	1 tsp. cinnamon
	1 tsp. GF pure vanilla
	3/4 tsp. GF pure almond extract
3/4 tsp. xanthan gum if using GF all purpose flour	12 cupcake liners

Preheat oven to 350°. Cook apples and mash them with 2 teaspoons of sugar and lemon juice. Process almonds to a fine texture. Combine flour, gum, cinnamon, processed almonds and 1/2 cup sugar in a bowl and stir with a whisk. Combine eggs, extracts and apple mash, stirring with a whisk. Add to flour mixture and lightly stir until just moistened. Spoon into 12 paper lined muffin pans. Bake at 350° for 20 to 22 minutes. Test with a toothpick to make sure that the center is baked through. Yield: 12 muffins

Banana Bread

- 1/2 C. tapioca flour
- 1/2 C. white rice flour
- 1/4 C. brown rice flour
- 1/4 C. sorghum flour
- 1/2 C. potato flour
- 1 tsp. xanthan gum
- 1 tsp. baking powder, see Two Flowers recipe
- 1 tsp. baking soda
- 1 tsp. cinnamon
- 1/2 tsp. nutmeg
- 1 tsp. salt
- 3/4 C. light brown sugar, packed
- 1 1/2 C. bananas, mashed, ripe
- 1/2 C. canola oil
- 1/4 C. whole milk
- 1 tsp. GF pure vanilla
- 2 eggs room temperature

Preheat oven to 350°. Stir together flours, gum and all other dry ingredients. Beat remaining ingredients until blended. Add flour mix and stir until mixed. Pour into a greased 9 x 5 loaf pan. Bake 30 minutes at 350° uncovered. Cover with foil and bake 25 minutes more. Cool completely before slicing. Yield: 1 loaf

Blueberry Muffins

- 3 C. + 1 T. GF muffin mix, see Two Flowers recipe
- 10 T. unsalted butter
- 3/4 C. sugar
- 2 large eggs
- 1 C. sour cream
- 1 T. lemon juice
- 1 tsp. lemon zest, grated
- 1 C. fresh blueberries

Preheat oven to 375°. In a mixer cream sugar with butter. Add eggs, sour cream and lemon juice. Toss the blueberries with 1 tablespoon of the flour and set aside. This will help keep the blueberries whole and not so mushy. Add remaining flour to creamed butter mixture. Mix. Stir in blueberries, trying not to break them up. Fill each muffin tin with a paper or silicone baking cup. Pour in the batter evenly among the 12 cups. Bake at 375° for 35 minutes. Yield: 12 to 18 muffins depending upon size

Buckwheat Pancakes

2 C. buckwheat flour
4 T. brown sugar
2 tsp. baking powder
1/4 tsp. salt
1/4 tsp. cinnamon
1/4 tsp. nutmeg
1/4 tsp. cloves, powdered
2 eggs
2 C. buttermilk
2 T. butter, melted
Canola oil to coat the pan

Whisk the dry ingredients together. Mix together the wet ingredients. Stir the dry ingredients into the wet ingredients. Lightly coat a griddle with oil. Use 1/4 cup of batter to make each pancake. Re-oil the griddle between frying batches. Yield: 8 servings

Buttermilk Biscuits

1 1/4 C. brown rice flour
1/4 C. tapioca flour
2 1/4 tsp. xanthan gum
2 tsp. baking powder, see Two Flowers recipe
1 tsp. baking soda
1/2 tsp. salt
1 T. sugar
1/2 C. unsalted butter, from the freezer, cut into cubes
2 eggs, beaten
1/3 C. buttermilk
GF cooking spray
1 T. melted unsalted butter to brush the biscuit tops

Preheat oven to 425°. To make buttermilk, add 1 teaspoon lemon juice to 1 cup of milk. Let it stand until it thickens. Line a cookie sheet with parchment paper and spray the paper. Sprinkle with a little of the GF flour. Combine all dry ingredients in a food processor and process to mix. Add butter and pulse until mixture resembles peas. Add egg and buttermilk. Process until the dough forms a ball. Put the dough onto the cookie sheet. Pat the dough into a 10 inch square with a 3/4 inch to 1 inch thickness. Cut the biscuits into 5 rolls down and 2 across. Rearrange biscuits on the cookie sheet so that there is space between the rolls. Brush the tops of rolls with melted butter. Bake for 15 minutes. Yield: 10 biscuits

Cheddar Sweet Sausage Muffins
A no-flour muffin

- 8 oz. GF Italian sweet sausage
- 2 C. broccoli, finely chopped
- 1 C. cheddar or Swiss cheese, shredded
- 1/4 C. sun-dried tomatoes, packed in oil, drained and chopped
- 1 tsp. fresh basil, slivered
- 1/2 tsp. onion powder
- 1/2 tsp. sea salt
- 8 eggs
- 1 T. fresh chives, chopped
- Unsalted butter to grease the muffin tins

Preheat oven to 350°. Grease a 1 12 cup muffin pan. Brown sausage and place sausaage into the bottom of each muffin cup. Cook broccoli and distribute evenly into each cup. Combine the rest of the ingredients to make a batter. Pour evenly into the muffin cups. Bake for 30 minutes in a 350° oven until golden brown. Loosen the edges of each muffin before lifting them out. Yield: 12 muffins.

Cheesy Bacon Quick Bread

- 1 C. Parmesan cheese, shredded
- 1/2 C. sharp cheddar cheese, cubed
- 1/2 C. Gruyere cheese, cubed
- 3 C. GF all purpose flour, see Two Flowers recipe
- 2 1/4 tsp. xanthan gum
- 1 T. baking powder, see Two Flowers recipe
- 1/4 tsp. cayenne pepper
- 1 tsp. sea salt
- 1/4 tsp. ground pepper
- 1 1/4 C. whole milk
- 1 egg, beaten
- 1/4 C. sour cream
- 5 slices bacon, cooked crisp, reserve 3 tablespoons of bacon fat for bread
- 1/2 C. sweet onion, chopped
- GF pure cooking spray

Preheat oven to 350°. Spray a 9 x 5 loaf pan with cooking spray. Sprinkle 1/2 cup of Parmesan cheese in the bottom of the pan. Sauté the onion in the bacon fat. Set aside. In a large bowl whisk the dry ingredients and seasonings. Mix in the cheddar and Gruyere cheeses. Add the bacon and onion to the cheese mixture. In another bowl mix the sour cream, egg and milk together. Mix the wet ingredients into the dry ingredients to form a thick batter. Pour the batter into the prepared loaf pan, smoothing it out with a spatula. Top with the remaining 1/2 cup Parmesan cheese. Bake at 350° for 45 to 50 minutes. Test the center with a toothpick to make sure it is fully baked.

Chocolate Marble Bread with Ganache

1 C. unsalted butter, softened
1 1/2 C. GF all purpose flour, see Two Flowers recipe
3/4 tsp. xanthan gum
1/2 tsp. salt
3/4 tsp. baking powder, see Two Flowers recipe

8 oz. semisweet chocolate, chopped
2/3 C. sugar
4 large eggs
1/2 C. milk
1/2 tsp. GF pure vanilla
1/4 C. whipping cream

Preheat oven 350°. Butter a 9 x 5 loaf pan. Sift flour, salt, and baking powder. Melt 5 ounces of chocolate over simmering water. You can melt in the microwave but you must be watchful as chocolate burns quickly. Whip butter in a mixer until softened. Reserve the remaining 3 ounces of chocolate. Add sugar to the melted chocolate and continue to beat until fluffy. Add vanilla and eggs one at a time. Keep beating. Whisk gum and GF flour together and add to the egg/butter mixture a little at a time alternating with milk. Separate half the batter and add half of it to the chocolate mixture. Now you have a chocolate batter and a vanilla batter. Alternating the batter pour into 2 layers in the loaf pan. When all the batter is used run a table knife through the batter to marbleize it. Bake at 350° for 45 minutes. Heat whipping cream and pour it over the reserved chocolate in a bowl. Stir until smooth. Let the chocolate mixture stand to thicken. Pour over cooled bread.

Cinnamon-Raisin Yeast Rolls
Worth a little effort

Dough:
- 2 T. unsalted butter
- 1/4 C. sugar
- 2/3 C. warm milk, 100° to 110°
- 1 pkg. yeast
- 1 large beaten egg
- 1/4 C. canola oil
- 1/4 C. potato starch, not potato flour
- 3/4 C. cornstarch
- 1/2 C. white rice flour
- 1/4 tsp. baking soda
- 2 1/2 tsp. xantham gum
- 2 tsp. baking powder, see Two Flowers recipe
- 1/2 tsp. salt
- 1 tsp. GF pure vanilla

Filling:
- 1 C. light brown sugar
- 2 1/2 T. cinnamon
- 1/8 tsp. salt
- 1/3 C. unsalted butter
- 1 C. golden raisins, optional
- 1 C. nuts, optional

Icing:
- 8 T. unsalted butter
- 1 1/2 C. powdered sugar
- 1/4 C. cream cheese
- 1/2 tsp. GF pure vanilla

Preheat oven to 400°. Dissolve yeast in the warm milk. Temperature is important, too hot and the yeast will die, too cold and the dough will not rise. Beat egg, oil, and vanilla together. Add to milk mixture. Whisk all the remaining ingredients except optional raisins and nuts. Add this to the wet mixture and mix in a mixer until a dough forms. With your hands form the dough into a round dough ball. Put the dough ball into a greased bowl in a warm spot and let it rise for 60 minutes. Between 2 pieces of parchment paper roll out the dough into a 13 inch square, about 1/2 inch thick. Remove the top sheet from the dough. Mix filling ingredients and spread over the top of dough leaving a small edge without filling. Sprinkle raisins and nuts if you are using them on top. Use the paper to roll up the dough tightly. Start at the side that has the filling and end at the side that has no filling. This roll will resemble a log. Cut the log into 8 slices. Sprinkle cinnamon sugar on the bottom of either a round or square buttered baking pan. Sprinkle cinnamon sugar on the bottom of the pan. Arrange the cut rolls in the pan. It doesn't matter if some touch. Bake at 400° for 18 minutes. Cool. Prepare icing and ice the rolls. Yield: 8 to 10 rolls depending on your cutting size

Clover Leaf Dinner Rolls

1/2 C. warm water, 105° to 115°	3/4 C. potato starch
1 tsp. Knox gelatin	2 large eggs, room temperature
2 1/4 tsp. fast rising yeast	1/2 C. whole milk
1/2 C. sorghum flour	1/4 C. honey
1/2 C. brown rice flour	3 T. canola oil
1/2 C. white rice flour	1 tsp. apple cider vinegar
1/3 C. tapioca flour	2 tsp. xanthan gum
1/2 C. garbanzo flour	1 1/2 tsp. salt
3/4 C. cornstarch	

Preheat oven to 375°. Mix gelatin and yeast with water. Stir together flours and starches. Use processor for eggs, milk, honey, oil, gum, vinegar and salt. Process until blended. Add flour and yeast mixture and process until mixed. Form each roll from 3 small balls. Put 3 dough balls in each greased muffin pan. Cover with a piece of plastic wrap and let rise in a warm place until double in size. Bake at 375° for 14 to 16 minutes until light golden brown. Yield: 12 rolls

Cornbread

3/4 C. cornmeal	1/2 tsp. xanthan gum
1/2 C. tapioca flour	1 1/4 C. whole milk
1/4 C. white rice flour	1 tsp. cider vinegar
1/4 C. sorghum flour	1/3 C. honey
1/4 C. potato starch	2 eggs, room temperature
2 T. baking powder, see Two Flowers recipe	1/4 C. unsalted butter, melted
1 tsp. baking soda	1 C. blueberries, optional
1 tsp. salt	GF pure spray or unsalted butter to grease the pan

Preheat oven to 375°. Stir together all dry ingredients. Set aside. With an electric mixer beat together all liquids until foamy. Gradually add melted butter. Add cornmeal mixture to liquids and beat on low until blended. Fold in blueberries for a blueberry cornbread. Pour into a greased 8 inch square baking dish. Bake at 375° for 20 minutes or until the cornbread releases from the side of pan. Cool slightly and serve warm.

Cranberry-Nut Bread

1/3 C. orange juice
1 T. orange zest
2/3 C. buttermilk
6 T. unsalted butter, melted
1 egg
2 C. GF all purpose flour, see Two Flowers recipe
1 1/2 tsp. xanthan gum
1/2 C. sugar
1/2 C. brown sugar, lightly packed
1 tsp. salt
1 tsp. baking powder, see Two Flowers recipe
1/4 tsp. baking soda
1 1/2 C. fresh cranberries, chopped
1/3 C. walnuts or pecans, toasted

Preheat oven to 375°. Grease bottom of 9 x 5 inch loaf pan. In a small bowl, stir together the butter, egg, and buttermilk. Whisk together all dry ingredients except cranberries and nuts. Stir the liquid ingredients into the dry ingredients with a fork. Stir in the cranberries and nuts. Spread the batter into the loaf pan and bake for 20 minutes at 375°. Reduce the heat to 350° and bake until the toothpick comes out clean from the center, about 40 to 45 more minutes. Cool in the pan for a few minutes before loosening the sides. Cool at least an hour before cutting.

Crispy Parmesan Shells

Use this as a base for your favorite filling or salad instead of phyllo dough or puff pastry.

3 C. Parmesan cheese, shredded, not grated

Preheat oven to 375°. Spread Parmesan cheese on a cookie sheet into a 6 x 12 inch rectangle. Bake at 375° for 5 minutes or more until the cheese is melted into a solid piece. While hot cut into eight 3 inch squares. Bake these squares until golden, about 4 more minutes. Remove from oven and press each square into muffin tins to shape them into cups. Let cool. Replaces a savory tart shell. Yield: 8 muffin sized shells

Frenchy Crepe Pancakes
Nana (Gladys Nosse)

- 4 T. oil for frying
- 1 1/4 C. milk
- 2 large eggs
- 2 T. unsalted butter, melted
- 1 C. GF all purpose flour, see Two Flowers recipe
- 1/2 tsp. salt
- 1 tsp. sugar
- 1/2 tsp. vanilla
- 1/8 tsp. baking powder

Cheese filling:
- 2 C. ricotta cheese or small curd cottage cheese
- 3 oz. cream cheese
- Zest of 1 lemon
- 3 T. powdered sugar
- 1 egg

Topping: fresh fruit or sauce of choice

Make wax paper squares to stack between the crepes before filling. Mix all ingredients except oil in a blender. Use 1/4 cup batter for each crepe. Spread batter to 1/4 inch thickness on a greased, 7 to 8 inch fry pan. Use 1/4 teaspoon oil to grease the pan for each crepe. Brown crepe on one side only. Tap crepe out on a sheet of waxed paper. Fill crepe with 1/8 cup cheese filling on the uncooked side. Roll it up so the browned side is showing. Put rolled crepes in baking dish, seam down and bake for 10 minutes. Dust with powdered sugar and top with fruit or warmed jam. Yield: 8 crepes

Golden Waffles

- 1 C. brown rice flour
- 1/2 C. potato starch
- 1/4 C. tapioca flour
- 2 tsp. baking powder
- 1 tsp. salt
- 1 tsp. sugar
- 1/4 C. canola oil
- 2 eggs
- 1 1/2 C. buttermilk
- 1 tsp. vanilla

Whisk all the dry ingredients together. Beat the eggs, add oil, milk and vanilla. Add the liquids to the dry ingredients. Follow your directions for your waffle maker. Yield: 5 waffles

Hash Brown Crust

Use this savory crust in place of a regular crust for dinner or brunch offerings such as quiche typically made with pie crust

3 C. GF frozen hash brown potatoes, shredded variety
2 T. unsalted butter, melted
1/2 tsp. sea salt
1/4 tsp. pepper

Thaw potatoes and toss with salt and pepper. Brush the butter on the bottom and sides of a pie plate or the bottom of muffin tins. The muffin tin will produce smaller crusts. Pat the thawed potatoes, making a crust, in the pie plate or muffin tin. Fill with your favorite quiche filling and bake according to your quiche directions.

Kalamata Olive Bread

1 T. olive oil
1 C. onion, minced
2 C. GF all purpose flour, see Two Flowers recipe
1 1/2 tsp. xanthan gum
1 tsp. baking soda
1/2 tsp. salt
1 C. buttermilk
2 T. unsalted butter, melted
2 large egg whites
1/2 C. Kalamata olives, drained and chopped
1 T. fresh basil, chopped
1/4 tsp. salt
1/8 tsp. pepper
GF pure cooking spray

Preheat oven to 350°. Sauté onion in oil until tender. Combine dry ingredients and whisk. With the back of a cup make a well in the center of flour mixture. Add combined wet ingredients to flour and stir until moist. Add onions, olives and basil. Spread batter into a sprayed 9 X 5 loaf pan. Pour batter into pan and bake at 350° for 45 minutes, uncovered. Cool and remove from pan.

Lemon Bread with Lemony Glaze

Bread:
1/2 C. unsalted butter
1 C. sugar
2 eggs
2 T. fresh lemon juice
1 T. lemon zest
1/2 C. rice flour
1/2 C. almond flour
1/2 C. tapioca flour
1 tsp. xanthan gum
1 tsp. baking powder, see Two Flowers recipe
1/8 tsp. salt
1/2 C. milk
1 tsp. GF pure vanilla

Glaze:
2 T. fresh lemon juice
1/4 C. powdered sugar
1/2 tsp. lemon zest

Preheat oven to 350°. Sift all dry ingredients together. Set aside. With an electric mixer beat butter until fluffy. Add sugar and continue to beat until batter is fluffy and light yellow in color. Gradually add flour mixture alternating with liquids and continue to beat on medium until batter is fully incorporated. Spoon into a buttered 9 X 5 loaf pan and bake for 55 minutes. Cool and invert on a serving plate.

Glaze: Add lemon juice and zest to powdered sugar by making a well in the center of the sugar and adding the lemon juice. Stir well until you can spoon the mixture over the warm cake. Sprinkle a few threads of zest over the glaze.

Pasta Dough
This noodle dough is so easy you will be done before you read the recipe

1 C. brown rice flour
1 C. tapioca flour
1 1/2 tsp. xanthan gum
3 eggs

1/4 tsp. salt
1/8 tsp. black pepper
pinch of nutmeg

I make a double recipe but make each recipe separately into 2 dough balls. It is so much easier to work with 1 dough ball at a time. Beat eggs and set aside. Whisk the 2 flours and the gum together in a bowl. Make a well in the center of the flour and add egg mixture. Incorporate with your fingers the wet ingredients into the dry ingredients. Form a glossy ball. Using tapioca flour on the surface, roll out the dough to about 1/8 inch thickness. Cut the rolled dough into the size noodle you would prefer. You can even cut very fine noodles or lasagna noodles. Boil the noodles in broth or hot water for 5 minutes. Fresh, gluten free noodles boil much quicker than wheat noodles. Yield: 4 dinner sized servings.

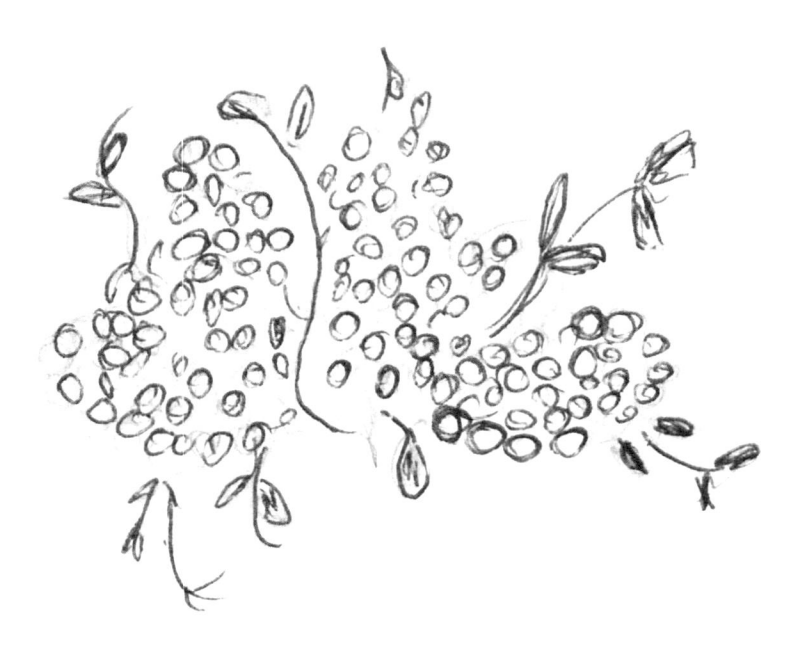

Pepper Jack Cheese Pancakes
Serve with a salsa from our Sauces and Dressings category

- 2 C. yellow cornmeal
- 1 C. GF all purpose flour, see Two Flowers recipe
- 1/2 tsp. xanthan gum
- 1 T. baking powder, see Two Flowers recipe
- 1 tsp. salt
- 2/3 C. pepper jack cheese, shredded
- 2 1/2 C. milk
- 4 eggs, beaten
- 1/4 C. unsalted butter
- 3 T. sour cream
- Salsa
- Sour cream

Preheat oven to 225°. Line a cookie sheet with parchment paper or foil so you can keep pancakes warm in the oven. Whisk together the dry ingredients and mix in cheese. Mix together the milk, eggs, and melted butter. Add the milk mixture to the flour mixture. You should be able to pour the batter. If you need to thin the batter add more milk. Heat a griddle and brush pan with canola or vegetable oil. To make the pancakes use 1/4 cup of batter for each pancake. As you make each pancake, put them on the warmed cookie sheet in the oven. Put a dollop of salsa and sour cream on each pancake. Yield: 18 small pancakes.

Pie Crust
A must have recipe

1/2 C. butter, frozen	1/2 tsp. xanthan gum
1 egg	1 tsp. salt
2 T. ice water, with cubes	2 T. sugar
1/4 tsp. cider vinegar	
1 1/4 C. GF all purpose flour, see Two Flowers recipe	

Cut frozen slices of butter and put into the food processor. Add GF flour, gum, salt, and sugar. Add water and vinegar. Process until the dough forms small clumps. Only add more water if the dough does not stick together. Less water is better. Roll dough between 2 pieces of waxed paper or plastic wrap to fit a 9 inch pie plate. Proceed with your favorite pie filling. If you need a pre-baked shell prick the bottom and sides of the plate and fill it with beans or rice. The filler will allow the crust to bake without bubbling up. Bake the crust at 350° for 20 minutes. Pour out the beans/rice and bake for 10 minutes more. The crust should be golden in color. Cover the edges with foil so they do not brown too much. Cool and fill.

Pizz-a-ria Pizza Crust

1 pkg. instant dry yeast	1 tsp. cider vinegar
1 C. warm water, 110° to 115°	1 tsp. olive oil
1/2 C. sorgrum flour	1 tsp. dry basil
2 T. dry milk powder	1 tsp. sea salt
2 tsp. xanthan gum	1 tsp. sugar
1 tsp. basil	1 to 1 1/2 C. brown rice flour
1 tsp. unflavored gelatin	

Preheat oven to 425°. Dissolve yeast in warm water. Add all other ingredients to yeast mixture. Use only 2/3 cup brown rice flour for mix. Put this mixture into a mixing bowl and beat until smooth but sticky. Stir in enough brown rice flour to make a ball. Roll dough between 2 pieces of waxed paper to form a circle to fit your pizza pan. Transfer dough to a pizza pan greased with olive oil. Cover pan and let rest for 1 hour at room temperature. Bake at 425° for 10 to 12 minutes until light brown. Spread 1 tablespoon olive oil over the crust and add your toppings. Bake 15 minutes longer until toppings are light brown.

Raspberry Cornmeal Muffins

1/4 C. unsalted butter
2 eggs, beaten
1 1/2 C. buttermilk
1 1/2 C. yellow cornmeal
1/2 C. GF all purpose flour, see Two Flowers recipe
3/8 tsp. xanthan gum
2 tsp. baking powder, see Two Flowers recipe
1/2 tsp. baking soda
2 T. sugar
1 tsp. salt
1 tsp. orange zest
1 C. raspberries
3 T. seedless raspberry preserves
GF cooking spray

Preheat oven to 450°. Spray 12 muffin tins or line the muffin tins with baking cups. Melt butter and let it cool. Add eggs and milk to the butter. Set aside. Sift all the dry ingredients together into a bowl. Make a well in the flour mixture and pour the liquid into the center. Add the zest. Use a fork to mix the batter just until the dry ingredients are moistened. The batter should be lumpy. Fill the muffin tins 1/2 the way up. Put fresh raspberries into each cup and put a dollop of raspberry preserves on top of the berries. Spoon more batter over the raspberry filling. Fill about 2/3 of the way up. Bake at 450° for 15 minutes or until the tops are lightly browned. Serve from the oven. Yield: 12 muffins

Rice Crust for Quiche or Pies

3/4 C. white or brown rice; do not use seasoning package if you are using rice from a box
1 1/2 C. water
1 well beaten egg
1 T. Parmesan or Romano cheese, grated, omit cheese for fruit pies

Preheat oven to 425°. Cook rice using above proportions of rice to water until tender according to directions on the package. Drain rice. Mix rice with egg and cheese. Press into pie plate forming a crust. Bake for 5 minutes at 425°. Remove from oven and cool on a wire rack. Proceed with a GF quiche or pie recipe of your choice.

Rosemary Focaccia Bread

- 1 T. yeast
- 3 T. warm water 100° to 115°
- 1 C. sorghum flour
- 1/4 C. cornstarch
- 1/4 C. brown rice flour
- 1 T. xanthan gum
- 4 T. canola oil
- 2 T. honey
- 1/2 C. whole milk
- 1/4 tsp. salt
- 1 egg, beaten
- 1 T. olive oil
- 1 T. salt
- 1 T. crushed dried basil leaves for topping
- 1 T. crushed dried rosemary for topping
- 1/2 C. sorghum flour for kneading

Preheat oven to 375°. In a bowl, dissolve yeast in warm water. Stir together all dry ingredients. Combine all wet ingredients except egg. Add wet ingredients to yeast. Add egg. Gradually add flour mixture. Stir quickly with a wooden spoon for at least 1 minute. Cover the bowl with a towel and put dough in a warm place to rise for 30 minutes. Dust your counter-top or cutting board with sorghum flour. Turn out the dough on the prepared surface and knead. Add extra flour if the dough becomes sticky. Flatten the dough into a puffy round and put on a greased parchment paper lined cookie sheet. Cover again with plastic wrap. Put in a warm place to rise for 1 hour. Brush the top of loaf with olive oil and sprinkle with basil and rosemary. Bake for 15 to 20 minutes at 375°. It should be a golden brown color. Cut into wedges to enjoy warm.

Shortcake Biscuits
Perfect for your fresh berries

2 1/2 C. GF all purpose flour, see Two flowers recipe
1 tsp. xanthan gum
4 tsp. baking powder, see Two Flowers recipe
1/2 tsp. salt

1/4 C. light brown sugar, packed
1/4 C. unsalted butter, frozen, cut into small slices
3/4 C. cream or milk
1/8 tsp. GF pure vanilla
GF pure cooking spray

Preheat oven to 350°. Pulse dry ingredients in a food processor. Add butter and continue to process until the mix becomes "sandy". Add milk and vanilla. Combine until the mixture actually becomes dough. Turn out on a GF floured board. With your hands form a ball and flatten the dough with the palm of your hand. Roll dough out into a circle to a 3/4 inch thickness. Dip a 3 inch or 4 inch cookie cutter in GF flour and use it to form the biscuit. Brush the biscuit tops with milk. Put them on a parchment lined, sprayed cookie sheet and bake at 350° until light brown. Yield: 12 biscuits

Southern Spoonbread
Is it a souffle or a corn bread?

4 1/2 C. whole milk
1 1/2 C. cornmeal
2 tsp. baking powder, see Two Flowers recipe
1 1/2 tsp. salt

1/8 tsp. nutmeg
3 T. unsalted butter, cold
6 eggs, separated
1/2 C. sharp cheddar cheese, shredded

Preheat oven to 400°. Pour 4 cups of milk into a saucepan and heat until the milk starts to bubble. Remove from heat. With a whisk, incorporate cornmeal into the milk. Heat and stir until it thickens. Add the rest of the milk. Cut the cold butter into the mixture. Add the salt, nutmeg and stir until the butter is melted. Add eggs yolks, one at a time to the mixture. Keep stirring after each egg is added. Stir in the baking powder. With an electric mixer beat all the whites until they are stiff and dry. Start folding the whites into the cornmeal mixture, a little at a time. When all the whites are folded in, pour them into a greased 3 quart baking dish. Bake until puffed and golden in color. Test the with a toothpick after 45 minutes. The toothpick should come out clean. Serve warm. Yield: 10 servings

Sweet Italian Sausage Quick Bread

- 1/2 C. unsalted butter
- 1/8 tsp. powdered sage
- 8 oz. sweet Italian sausage
- 1 T. canola oil
- 1 1/2 C. GF all purpose flour, see Two Flowers recipe
- 1 tsp. xanthan gum
- 1 T. sugar
- 1 T. baking powder, see Two Flowers recipe
- 1/2 tsp. salt
- 1 tsp. ground pepper
- 6 large eggs, room temperature
- 2 tsp. lemon peel, grated
- 3 oz. shredded cheese, the spicier the better
- 1/3 C. golden raisins, chopped
- 1 oz. Parmesan cheese, shredded, not grated

Preheat oven to 350°. Melt butter and let cool. Cook sausage without the casings, breaking the meat into small pieces. Cool sausage. Butter a 9 x 5 loaf pan. Sift together all the dry ingredients. Whisk eggs and lemon in a large bowl. Stir into dry ingredients. Add butter. Fold in sausage and cheeses. Pour the batter into the prepared loaf pan. Bake about 30 minutes until center of the bread comes out dry when tested with a toothpick.

Sweet Potato Bread
Very sweet and moist bread

- 1 3/4 C. GF all purpose flour, see Two Flowers recipe
- 3/4 tsp. xanthan gum
- 1 C. sugar
- 2 tsp. cinnamon
- 1 tsp. nutmeg
- 1 tsp. ground ginger
- 1/2 tsp. baking soda
- 1/2 tsp. baking powder, see Two Flowers recipe
- 1/2 tsp. salt
- 2 eggs
- 1 C. sweet potatoes, mashed, do not use yams
- 1/2 C. canola oil
- 1/3 C. orange juice
- 1 C. pecans, chopped, optional

Preheat oven to 350°. Mix all dry ingredients. Combine eggs, sweet potatoes, oil, and orange juice in a bowl. Stir into the dry ingredients until moistened. Spoon into a greased and GF floured 9 x 5 loaf pan. You can also line the bottom with wax paper. Sprinkle top lightly with a little sugar. Bake at 350° uncovered for 1 hour. Check with a toothpick to make sure the center is done. The toothpick will come out clean. Cool before removing loaf to a rack.

Tea Bread
A Trifles Cafe favorite, now gluten free

- 1/4 C. golden raisins
- 1 C. sugar
- 2 large eggs
- 1/2 C. applesauce
- 1 tsp. GF pure vanilla
- 2 C. GF all purpose baking flour, see Two Flowers recipe
- 1 1/2 tsp. baking powder, see Two Flowers recipe
- 2 tsp. xanthan gum
- 3/4 tsp. salt
- 2 tsp. cinnamon
- 1 tsp. nutmeg
- 1 C. carrots, shredded
- 1 C. zucchini, shredded
- 1/4 C. pineapple, crushed, drained
- 1/2 C. walnuts, chopped, optional
- 1/3 C. canola oil

Preheat oven to 350°. Cream oil, sugar, eggs and add applesauce. Stir in nuts, raisins, and raw vegetables. Fill 2 9 x 5 inch greased loaf pans and bake at 350° uncovered for 60 minutes. Check with a toothpick to see if the center is done. The toothpick should come out clean. Cover the tops of the loaves with foil for the last 10 minutes to keep it from browning too much.

White Bread
Not so difficult

- 2 1/2 tsp. yeast
- 1 C. water warmed to 100° to 110°
- 1/4 C. honey
- 1/4 C. canola oil
- 1 large egg
- 1 tsp. cider vinegar
- 1 tsp. salt
- 1 1/3 C. white rice flour
- 1/4 C. potato flour
- 1/4 C. tapioca flour
- 1/4 C. potato starch
- 2 tsp. xanthan gum
- 1/3 C. milk
- 1 egg yolk

Preheat oven to 375°. Combine liquids except water. Set aside. Combine all dry ingredients except yeast. Set aside. Dissolve yeast in water. Add dissolved yeast into the rest of liquids in an electric mixing bowl. Mix everything together in the mixer and beat for 2 minutes. On a counter or cutting board, sprinkle any GF flour on the surface. Knead the dough until it is smooth and elastic about 5 minutes. Cover with a cloth and let dough rest 10 minutes. Shape into a loaf and put on a buttered cookie sheet. Cover and let rise until doubled in size. Brush with an egg yolk. Bake at 375° until browned about 45 minutes.

Make Your Own Mixes & Pantry Staples

Almond Granola
Kara Koprowski

1/2 C. packed light brown sugar
1/2 C. canola oil
2 tsp. GF pure vanilla
2 tsp. coarse sea salt
4 C. GF oats
1 C. almond slices
1/2 C. sunflower seeds, pepitas or pumpkin seeds
1 tsp. cinnamon
1 C. dried fruit of choice such as blueberries or cherries

Preheat oven to 350°. Line 2 baking sheets with foil trimmed to fit baking sheets. In a bowl whisk brown sugar, oil, and vanilla. Add oats, almonds, nuts and cinnamon. Make sure the mixture is well coated. Divide mixture between prepared pans. Sprinkle with kosher salt. Bake in 350° oven until golden, approximately 20 minutes. Toss twice. Add dried fruit after baking. Let cool completely before storing in air tight container. You may also add sweetened flaked coconut in place of some of the dried fruit. Yield: 6 cups and lasts 2 weeks.

All Purpose Flour Mix

3 C. brown rice flour
3 C. white rice flour
2 C. potato starch, not potato flour
1 C. tapioca flour

Use in place of wheat flour as an equal substitution in recipes. Whisk together and store in an air tight container. Yield: 4 1/2 cups Depending on your use you will need to add xanthan gum to your baked goods to bind the flours. The simple chart that follows is suggested by Bob's Red Mill flour products.
Per cup of GF flour add the following:
1/4 tsp. for cookies
1/2 tsp. for cakes
3/4 tsp. for muffins and quick breads
1 to 1 1/2 tsp. for yeast bread
2 tsp. for pizza crust

Baking Powder
Aluminium free

1/4 tsp. baking soda
1/2 tsp. cream of tartar
1/4 tsp. cornstarch

Sift the ingredients together to make 1 teaspoon baking powder. By using this mix there will be no metallic taste in your baked products.

Bisquick Baking Mix Substitute

2 1/2 C. white rice flour
2/3 C. potato starch
3 T. baking powder, see Two Flowers recipe
2 tsp. sea salt
2 T. sugar
1/2 C. dry buttermilk powder
3 T. powdered egg substitute
3/4 C. + 3 T. unsalted butter

Whisk dry ingredients and cut in the butter until the mix is fine but not like sand! Store in the refrigerator. There are many Betty Crocker GF recipes using GF Bisquick. No additives in this one!

Breading Choices

Almond meal
Ground nuts
GF crushed cereal
Stale GF bread crumbs
Dehydrated potato flakes
Crushed potato chips
Crushed rice crackers
1 egg
1 tsp. water
1 C. rice flour

Preheat oven to 400°. These are instructions for breading. Put 1 cup rice flour in a plate. Mix 1 egg with 1 teaspoon of water in another plate. Dip fish, vegetable, chicken, or pork in flour first. Shake excess off, then dip into egg mixture. End by dipping into breading choice. You can either fry or oven bake entree at 400°.

Brown Sugar

1 C. sugar
1 1/2 T. GF molasses, for light brown sugar
1/4 C. GF molasses, for dark brown sugar

Combine sugar and molasses to make light or dark brown sugar. Measure what you need from this mixture. Store tightly covered.

Cajun Seasoning

2 tsp. salt
2 tsp. garlic powder
2 1/2 tsp. paprika
1 tsp. pepper
1 tsp. onion powder
1 tsp. cayenne pepper
1 1/4 tsp. oregano
1 1/4 tsp. dried thyme
1/2 tsp. red pepper

Whisk all the ingredients together and store in a covered jar.

Classic Dry Chili Mix
Good to have on hand

1 C. GF all purpose flour, see Two Flowers recipe
3/4 C. onion, dried, minced
4 T. chili powder
1/4 C. paprika
2 T. salt
1 T. cumin
1 T. garlic, dried, minced
1 T. sugar
1/2 tsp. cayenne pepper

Combine and divide into batches of 1/2 cup each. Each seasoning pack will season 1 pound of ground beef. Yield: 4 1/2 cup seasoning packets

Crumble Topping for Pies, Muffins and Cobblers

- 1 C. G.F. all purpose flour, see Two Flowers recipe
- 1/2 C. sugar
- 1/4 C. brown sugar, see Two Flowers recipe
- 1 tsp. salt
- 1/2 tsp. xanthan gum
- 6 T. unsalted butter, chilled, cut into small cubes
- 1 tsp. cinnamon

Blend all ingredients in blender, except butter. When blended, pulse the butter into mixture until it resembles sand. Add to the top of your favorite cobbler, muffin or pie and bake according to your recipe's directions.

Dry Meat Rub
A test kitchen best!

- 8 tsp. brown sugar
- 8 tsp. paprika
- 4 tsp. dry mustard
- 4 tsp. coarse pepper
- 4 tsp. onion flakes, granulated
- 4 tsp. sea salt
- 2 tsp. garlic powder
- 2 tsp. ground cumin
- 1 tsp. cayenne pepper
- 4 T. orange peel, optional

Break up any lumps. Mix and store half the amount. The orange peel gives it extra zing. Yield: enough rub for 10 pounds of meat. Make a full recipe and store half of the recipe for later use.

Herb de Provence
Classic French herb mixture to flavor any fish, meat, or vegetable

2 T. each:
Rosemary
Thyme
Parsley
Oregano
Fennel seeds
Marjoram

Savory
1 T. each:
Sage
Basil
Dried lavender, optional herb
1 bay leaf

Put all dried herbs in a jar with a lid. Shake well. Store for up to 4 months away from the heat. Yield: 1 1/4 cups

Hot Cocoa Mix

3 C. dry milk
2 C. powdered sugar
1 1/2 C. cocoa powder
1 1/2 C. semisweet chocolate chips
1/4 tsp. salt

Mix together and store in airtight jar. Use 1/3 cup to 1/2 cup for 1 cup of milk to make a cup of cocoa. Top with whipped cream or marshmallows or both!

Magic Seasoning
Sprinkle on everything

15 garlic cloves, peeled
1 C. coarse salt
1 1/2 tsp. onion powder
1 T. paprika
1 tsp. pepper
1 1/2 tsp. ground ginger
1 1/2 tsp. celery seed
1 1/2 tsp. dry mustard
1 T. dried dill
1 1/2 tsp. dried chives

In a food processor, mince the garlic. In a measuring cup combine all the other ingredients and pour them into the processor. Pulse until blended. Store in the refrigerator in a glass jar.

Methods for Cooking Dried Beans

1 lb. any type of dried beans
10 C. water

No need to soak lentils, split peas, or black-eyed peas

Quick Soak Method:
Sort beans for stones. Rinse the beans. Combine 1 pound of beans with 10 cups of water in a large pot. Bring beans and water to a boil. Let them boil for 2 minutes. Remove from heat, cover, let them stand for 1 hour. Rinse and drain again. They are now ready to cook.

Overnight Soak:
Sort beans for stones. Rinse the beans. Combine 1 pound of beans with 10 cups of water in a large pot. Let them stand in the water 6 to 8 hours, or overnight. Rinse and drain. They are now ready to cook.

Cooking Beans:
Return drained and rinsed beans to the pot and add 6 cups of water. Do not salt the water as that will toughen them. Bring beans to a boil. Simmer and cook beans until tender. This will take anywhere from 1 to 2 hours depending on the type of bean. Do not overcook. You do not want mushy beans. Use what you need for a recipe and freeze the rest in 2 cup containers. 2 cups of cooked dried beans will equal 15 ounces of canned beans. 1 pound dried beans will yield about 3 cups cooked beans.

Muffin Mix
You choose the additions.

2 1/4 C. brown rice flour
1/2 C. potato starch
1/2 C. tapioca flour
1 tsp. baking soda

4 tsp. baking powder
1 tsp. sea salt
1 tsp. xanthan gum
Your choice of additions

Mix well and store in an airtight container. This mix will serve as a basic flour mix for all muffins.
Yield: 4 to 8 muffins or more depending on additions.

Onion Soup Mix
Use this in place of dry onion soup mix

8 tsp. dried onion flakes
1 1/2 tsp. dried parsley
1 tsp. onion powder
1/2 tsp. celery seed
1/4 tsp. pepper
1/8 tsp. garlic powder
4 tsp. GF beef granules, Herb-Ox, low sodium

Mix all ingredients and store in a jar or freezer bag. This mix equals 1 package of onion soup by adding 4 cups of water. This mix is saltless, except for the beef granules, so add salt to taste if needed. Most packaged soup mixes are loaded with salt.

Pancake Mix

1 C. white rice flour
3 T. tapioca flour
1/3 C. potato starch, not flour
4 T. dry buttermilk
2 tsp. sugar
1 1/2 tsp. baking powder, see Two Flowers recipe
1/2 tsp. baking soda
1/2 tsp. sea salt
1/2 tsp. xanthan gum
You can triple this mix and store for later use

To make a basic pancake just add 2 eggs, 3 tablespoons of canola oil, 1 teaspoon vanilla and 2 cups of water for a batch of pancakes. Put in your own additions. I put the batter down in 3 inch circles. Add fruit etc. to the actual pancake. You get just what you want where you want it! This is a good pancake mix to use with any pancake recipe.

Pastry Flour
Use for cakes, bars and cookies but not breads

3 C. brown rice flour
1 C. potato starch, not flour
1/2 C. tapioca flour
1 1/4 tsp. xanthan gum

In food processor, pulse brown rice flour until it is a fine grind. Sift together the potato starch, tapioca flour and xanthan gum. Add to the brown rice flour. Store in freezer. Use at room temperature for baking. This flour mixture can be interchanged in any of your favorite bar, cake or cookie recipe for the wheat equivalent. Yield: 4 1/2 cups

Poultry Seasoning

2 C. dry parsley
1/2 C. sage
1/2 C. dried rosemary, crushed
1/2 C. marjoram
2 T. sea salt

1 T. black pepper
2 tsp. onion flakes
1 ground bay leaf
1 tsp. paprika

Combine all the ingredients and store in a jar with a lid or a plastic bag.

Self- Rising Cornmeal Mix

3/4 C. yellow cornmeal
3 T. GF all purpose flour, see Two Flowers recipe

1 T. baking powder, see Two Flowers recipe
1/2 tsp. sea salt

Combine all ingredients and store in a glass jar. Use this mix in any recipe calling for self-rising cornmeal.

Self- Rising Flour

Can be substituted in any recipe calling for a self rising flour

1 C. GF all purpose flour, see Two Flowers recipe
1 1/2 tsp. baking powder, see Two Flowers recipe

1/2 tsp. sea salt

Whisk all ingredients together. Store in a jar or plastic bag. Use in place of purchased self rising flour.

Taco Seasoning

1 T. potato starch
2 T. GF. onion powder
2 tsp. GF garlic powder
1 T. sea salt
1 T. chili powder

1 1/2 tsp. crushed red pepper
1 1/2 tsp. ground cumin
1 tsp. ground oregano
1/4 tsp. sugar

Mix seasonings well and store in a bag or jar. This recipe plus 3/4 cup water will season 1 pound of raw meat.

Terrific "Breading"

2 C. white rice flour
2/3 C. potato starch
1/3 C. tapioca flour

1/2 C. milk
1 beaten egg

Use this coating for meat, poultry and fish. Use 2 shallow dishes to make a milk tray and an egg tray. Dip your protein choice into the flour mixture, then the beaten egg mixture. Dip both sides into the coating, patting it on. Proceed to bake on a parchment lined cookie sheet or fry according to your recipe directions.

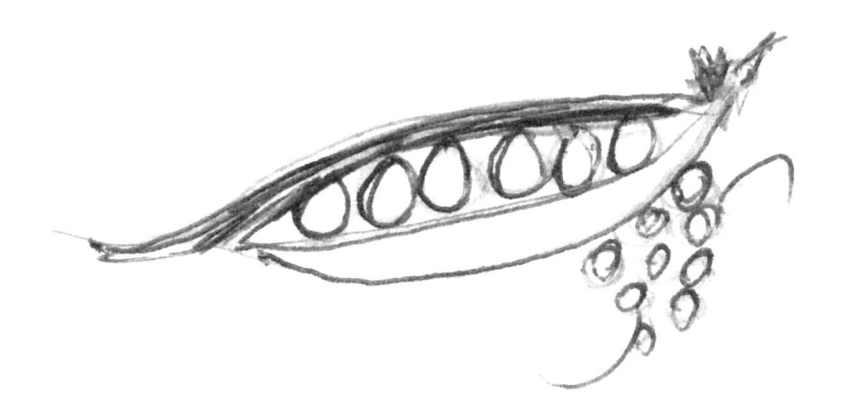

NOTES

Satisfying Meals

Asian Spicy Shrimp Noodle Bowl

- 1 lb. large shrimp, raw, peeled and deveined
- 1 1/2 C. water
- 1 1/2 C. GF chicken broth, see Two Flowers Recipe
- 1 8 oz. bottle clam juice
- 2 flat slices of fresh ginger, peeled
- 1 tsp. olive oil
- 1/2 C. red pepper, slivered
- 1/2 C. green pepper, slivered
- 1/2 C. whole snap peas, with ends trimmed
- 1/4 C. green onion, slivered
- 1 garlic clove, minced
- 1/2 tsp. crushed red pepper
- 1/4 tsp. sea salt
- 8 oz. uncooked rice stick noodles
- Light olive oil for frying
- Fresh lime slices for garnish

Cook shrimp in water, chicken broth and clam juice, about 8 to 10 minutes. Shrimp will turn pink when done. Remove shrimp and strain broth. Save the strained broth. In a large skillet or stir fry pan, heat oil. Sauté vegetables and seasonings except the snap peas for 3 minutes. Add reserved broth and simmer 3 to 5 minutes. Add cooked shrimp, snap peas and rice sticks. Cook until the noodles are done, about 5 to 8 minutes. Garnish with fresh lime. Yield: 4 servings

Baked Florentine Sole

- 2 T. unsalted butter
- 3 T. green onions, bulbs and tops, minced
- 1 garlic clove, minced
- 2 C. light cream
- 2 tsp. fresh thyme
- 4 tsp. cornstarch
- 1/2 tsp. sea salt
- 1/4 tsp. pepper
- 1/2 C. Parmesan cheese, grated
- 2 10 oz. pkg. frozen spinach, thawed and squeezed dry
- 1 1/2 lb. skinless sole fillets
- 3/4 C. GF rice crackers, finely crushed

Preheat oven to 475°. Melt 1 tablespoon of butter and spread it onto the bottom of a casserole dish. Melt 1 tablespoon of butter in a saucepan and cook the onions and garlic until soft. Stir in 1/2 the cream. Simmer to thicken. Dissolve the cornstarch into the remaining cream and whisk well. Simmer until the sauce thickens. Stir into the spinach 1 cup of the sauce and the Parmesan cheese. This will make the spinach filling. Pat the fillets dry. Separate the fillets on a cutting board, skin side up. Put the filling in the middle of the fillet. Fold the tail up tightly, then wrap the thicker part over and tuck under to make a nice firm roll. Put fillets with the seam side down in the casserole. Pour remaining sauce over the fillets and sprinkle with the rice cracker crumbs. Bake at 475° for 15 minutes, uncovered. Make sure the center of the fish is firm and not translucent. Yield: 6 servings

Beef Stroganoff Revisited

- 1 1/2 T. canola oil
- 1 1/2 C. white mushrooms. sliced
- 8 oz. beef tenderloin fillets
- 1 C. GF beef broth, see Two Flowers recipe
- 2 T. unsalted butter
- 1 C. sweet onion, minced
- 2 tsp. tomato paste
- 3 tsp. brown sugar
- 1/4 tsp. pepper
- 1/2 tsp. sea salt
- 1/8 tsp. nutmeg
- 2 tsp. fresh tarragon, minced
- 2 T. GF all purpose flour, see Two Flowers recipe
- 1 C. GF chicken broth, see Two Flowers recipe
- 1 C. white wine
- 2/3 C. sour cream
- GF noodles or rice

Cut tenderloin into 1/8 inch strips across the meat grain. Set aside. Heat oil in skillet. Add mushrooms and cook them for 1 minute. Add seasonings. Cook until mushrooms start to brown. Remove the mushrooms to a bowl. Spread the strips in skillet and cook for 2 minutes on each side until meat is well browned. Add the meat to the bowl with the mushrooms. Add beef broth to skillet scraping up all the meat bits. Reduce the broth to about 1/2 cup of liquid. Set aside. Add butter to skillet with tomato paste, onions, and brown sugar. Whisk in flour, chicken broth and white wine to the skillet. Add the reduced broth, reserving about 1/2 cup of the reduction. Whisk the reserved 1/2 cup of broth into the sour cream and heat to warm through. Do not boil! Pour the completed sauce over the meat and mushroom mixture. Cook GF noodles or rice according to package directions. Serve stroganoff over the cooked GF noodles or rice. Yield: 4 servings

Breakfast Bake
Kara Koprowski

- 1 20 oz. package fresh shredded hash brown potatoes, like Oreida
- 1 lb. GF bacon
- 2 C. GF ham, cubed or diced
- 3 C. cheese, shredded, cheddar and mozzarella mixed
- 1/2 medium sweet onion, diced
- 6 large eggs, beaten
- 2 C. milk
- 1 tsp. black pepper
- 1/8 tsp. dry mustard

Preheat oven to 350°. Brown bacon in skillet. Drain on paper towels, crumble, and set aside. Can also chop bacon coarsely before browning. Drain most of bacon grease from pan leaving a few tablespoons. Add onion to pan and sauté until onion begins to soften. Add hash brown potatoes and fry until the potatoes are starting to get some color, approximately 5 to 7 minutes. They should not be fully cooked. Lightly grease a 9 x 13 casserole dish. Layer half of the hash brown potato and onion mixture in prepared pan. Layer on top, 1/2 of the crumbled bacon and 1 cup of the ham. Spread 1 1/2 cup shredded cheese on top. Repeat layers with balance of hash brown potatoes, bacon, ham and cheese. Add spices to eggs and milk. Beat well and pour over the top of the casserole. Cover and refrigerate overnight. Bake covered with foil at 350° for 50 minutes. Turn off oven and let casserole sit in oven for 15 more minutes before serving. This recipe is fairly forgiving and easy to make vegetarian by adding sautéed vegetables in place of bacon and/or ham such as mushrooms, bell peppers, spinach or asparagus. If not using bacon or ham, you can add a 1 to 2 teaspoons salt to eggs. Yield: 6 to 8 servings

Bruschetta Chicken

1/2 C. GF all purpose flour, see Two Flowers recipe
1 large egg beaten
1 1/2 lb. chicken breasts
1/4 C. Parmesan cheese, shaved
1/4 C. GF bread crumbs
1 T. unsalted butter, melted
2 C. tomatoes, chopped, seeds removed
3 T. fresh basil, slivered
2 cloves garlic, minced
1 T. olive oil
1/2 tsp. salt
1/4 tsp. pepper

Preheat oven to 375°. Put flour and eggs in separate bowls. Dip chicken in flour, then eggs. Put chicken in a greased 9 x 13 pan. Combine cheese, bread crumbs and butter. Sprinkle this mixture over the chicken. Bake at 375° for 20 minutes, lightly covered. Uncover and bake to brown. Combine remaining ingredients. Spoon over chicken. Return to oven until tomato mixture is heated through. Yield: 4 servings

Cantonese Style Stir Fry
Kara Koprowski

4 T. vegetable or canola oil
3 C. sliced vegetables of choice:
Carrots
Mushrooms
Onions
Celery
Baby bok choy
Snow peas
Bell peppers
2 C. protein of choice:
Shrimp, peeled and deveined
Tofu, firm style, cubed
Pork
Chicken
Beef

1 recipe Two Flowers stir fry sauce:
Coconut Curry
Citrus Herb
Stir Fry
Cooked brown or white rice
Green onions, sliced, white and light green parts

Heat wok or other large stir fry pan to high heat. Add 2 tablespoons of oil and heat until hot. Vegetables will sizzle when added to the pan. Add vegetables and quickly stir fry for 3 to 4 minutes. Works best if vegetables are cut in similar sized pieces. If using harder vegetables such as carrots, make sure they are in small rounds or other bite sized pieces. Baby bok choy and snow peas will cook the quickest so stir fry last. Remove vegetables to a bowl and set aside. Add 2 tablespoons of oil to wok and heat until hot. Add protein and cook through, at least 3 to 4 minutes. Protein should be at room temperature. Best to slice diagonally or on the bias. Shrimp will cook faster and are cooked through when they are no longer translucent and turn pink. Add vegetables and one recipe of a Two Flowers stir fry sauce. Heat over low heat until combined. Or you can heat sauce separately and pour over protein and vegetables. Serve over cooked rice and sprinkle with green onion if desired.

You can make this dish vegetarian by using all vegetables. Just keep in mind the vegetable size and cooking times as you may need to add vegetables in stages to ensure all vegetables are cooked through but still crisp.

Cheesy Crab Bake

- 6 GF English muffins, Food for Life from Whole Foods is a great choice
- 8 oz. real lump crab meat, Phillips canned brand, if you are not using frozen or fresh
- 2 T. Dijon mustard
- 2 T. lemon juice
- 1 tsp. lemon peel, grated
- 2 C. sharp cheddar cheese, shredded
- 12 eggs
- 1 C. half and half
- 1 C. milk
- 1/2 C. GF mayonnaise, see Two Flowers recipe
- 1 tsp. sea salt
- 1/2 tsp. pepper
- 1/2 tsp. cayenne pepper
- 2 C. Swiss cheese, shredded
- 1 C. Parmesan cheese, grated
- 1/2 C. green onions, bulbs and tops, sliced
- 1/2 C. sweet peppers, chopped, use the colorful ones

Preheat oven to 375°. Spread mustard on the bottom halves of the muffins. Put muffins in a greased 9 x 13 casserole dish. Mix crab with lemon juice and lemon peel. Spread mixture on top of the prepared muffin bottom. Sprinkle with cheddar. Put the muffin top on. Whisk eggs with seasonings and mayonnaise. Pour this mixture over the muffins. Sprinkle with the two cheeses, onions and peppers.

Refrigerate overnight. Bring out casserole 30 minutes before baking. Cover with foil and bake at 375° for 30 minutes. Uncover and bake 20 minutes more, until custard is set. Let stand 10 minutes before serving. Yield: 8 to 12 servings

Chicken or Beef Enchiladas

- 2 lbs. grilled chicken or grilled beef, cut into 1/2" strips
- 2 tsp. olive oil
- 2 C. green onions, tops and bulbs, slivered
- 1/2 C. water
- 1 T. chili powder
- 1 1/2 tsp. cumin
- 1/2 tsp. sea salt
- 1/2 tsp. pepper
- 2 C. tomatoes, diced
- 1 4 oz. can green chilies, drained
- 1/4 C. black olives, sliced
- 8 oz. cream cheese
- 4 oz. cheddar cheese, shredded
- 2 oz. jack cheese, shredded
- Sour cream for topping

Preheat oven to 350°. Sauté onion in oil until tender. Mix half of the onion with cooked meat. Put water, chili powder, cumin, sea salt, pepper, tomatoes, and chilies in blender with the other half of the cooked onions and process until smooth. Set aside. Mix the cream cheese and 1/2 cup of the sauce mixture into meat. Spread 1/2 cup of tomato mixture on the bottom of a 9 x 13 pan. Heat remaining sauce in pan. Dip each corn tortilla into sauce. Working one at a time spoon 3 tablespoons of the meat filling onto each tortilla. Roll tortillas and place them in dish, seam side down. Pour remaining sauce over the top and sprinkle with cheeses. Bake uncovered for 30 minutes at 350°. Yield: 12 enchiladas. Serve with a tablespoon of sour cream on each enchilada.

Chicken Divan

- 3 1/2 C. cooked rice
- 5 C. broccoli florets, blanched
- 5 C. grilled chicken or pulled chicken
- 3 1/2 C. white sauce, see Two Flowers recipe
- 3/4 C. GF mayonnaise, see Two Flowers recipe
- 3/4 C. sour cream
- 1 1/4 C. cheddar cheese, shredded
- 1 T. fresh lemon juice
- 2 tsp. lemon zest
- Topping:
- 2 T. unsalted butter, melted
- 1 1/4 C. GF Corn Flakes or GF Rice Crispies finely processed

Preheat oven to 350°. Layer the ingredients in the following order: rice, sauce, broccoli, sauce, chicken, sauce in a greased 9 x 13 baking pan. Spread topping over the top. Bake uncovered 45 to 60 minutes at 350°. Yield: 8 servings

Chicken Paprikash with Noodles

- 3 yellow onions, sliced
- 2 T. unsalted butter
- 1 1/2 lbs. chicken bone-in-breasts and 4 chicken legs with thighs
- 2 tsp. sea salt
- 3/4 tsp. pepper
- 2 T. Hungarian paprika
- 1 tsp. dried thyme
- 1/2 tsp. cayenne pepper
- 2 bay leaves
- 1 lb. mushrooms, sliced
- 2 C. tomatoes, sliced and seeded
- 2 C. chicken broth, see Two Flowers recipe
- 3 tsp. cornstarch, dissolved in 2 T. cold water
- 1 C. sour cream
- 2 lbs GF noodles
- 4 T. parsley, chopped

Heat butter and cook onions. Remove onions from skillet and set aside. Sauté mushrooms in the skillet. Remove and set aside. Add chicken pieces to brown, after salt and peppering the pieces. Add the sliced onions to the browned chicken. Add dry spices, onions, tomatoes, garlic, mushrooms, and broth to skillet. Bring to a boil. Turn down heat and simmer for about 45 minutes covered. Remove from heat and stir in cornstarch mixture, stirring constantly. Stir in sour cream right before serving. Do not boil or the sour cream will curdle. Serve alone or with cooked GF noodles. Yield: 6 to 8 servings.

Chicken Stew with Dumplings

Stew:
- 2 qt. chicken broth, see Two Flowers recipe
- 4 C. chicken or turkey, cooked, shredded
- 2 C. carrots, chopped
- 1 C. celery, chopped
- 1 C. sweet onions, chopped
- 2 tsp. sea salt
- 2 tsp. thyme
- 1/2 tsp. pepper
- 2 bay leaves
- 1/2 C. cornstarch

Dumplings:
- 3/4 C. GF all purpose flour, see Two Flowers recipe
- 1/2 C. cornstarch
- 1/4 C. tapioca starch
- 1 T. baking powder, see Two Flowers recipe
- 1/2 tsp. sea salt
- 1 tsp. GF poultry seasoning, see Two Flowers recipe
- 1/8 tsp. xanthan gum
- 3/4 C. sour cream
- 3/4 C. chicken stock, see Two Flowers recipe
- 2 T. olive oil

Dissolve cornstarch in 1 cup of broth. Slowly add the rest of the broth to the cornstarch and stir until it starts to thicken. Add seasonings and simmer until carrots and onions are tender. Add cooked chicken or turkey.

Dumplings: Whisk all dry ingredients and seasonings. Add stock, sour cream and oil. Stir until blended. Use a 1/8 cup measuring cup for the dumpling size. Drop the dumplings onto the stew. Cover with lid and simmer for 20 minutes. Yield: 8 servings

Creamy Scrambled Eggs
So who can't make scrambled eggs?

- 8 eggs
- 3 oz. cream cheese, very cold, or use goat cheese if preferred
- 6 T. unsalted butter
- 2 T. fresh chives for garnish
- 1/4 tsp. sea salt
- 1/8 tsp. ground pepper
- Sour cream or Greek yogurt for garnish

Whisk eggs in bowl. Grate the near frozen cream cheese. Whisk the eggs and cheese together and add seasoning. Now here is the big secret. Using a double boiler melt the butter over simmering water. When the butter is melted pour in the egg mixture. Cook slowly, stirring all the time with the whisk. Spoon the eggs into serving dish and garnish with the sour cream and chives. Yield: 4 serviings

Crispy Chicken

3 C. GF Rice Krispies, crushed
1 tsp. paprika
1/2 tsp. sea salt
1/4 tsp. pepper
1 1/2 lbs. chicken breasts
1/2 C. GF mayonnaise

Preheat oven to 425°. Mix all ingredients in a plastic bag except mayonnaise. Brush mayonnaise on the chicken breasts, one piece at a time. Shake the chicken breast in the mixture in the plastic bag. Bake at 425° for 40 to 45 minutes, covered, until golden brown. Yield: 5 to 6 servings

Crock Pot Macaroni and Cheese

Kara Koprowski - this recipe makes a creamy baked mac and cheese with a golden crust in the crock pot.

8 oz. dry GF pasta, elbow, penne or rotelli shaped
4 C. cheddar cheese, shredded
1 12 oz. can evaporated milk
1 1/2 C. whole or low fat milk
1 stick unsalted butter, melted
2 well beaten large eggs
1 T. salt
1 T. fresh ground pepper
1 T. red pepper flakes

Reserve 1 cup of the cheddar cheese. Cook GF pasta according to package directions but "under cook" by 3 to 4 minutes. Drain. Pasta should be al dente and will finish cooking in the crock pot. Combine wet ingredients with 3 cups cheese, pasta, salt and pepper. Stir gently to combine. Sprinkle 1 cup of the reserved cheese on top. Cook on low for 3 to 4 hours. No longer than 4 hours or pasta will break down and cheese will burn. Do not peek or lift cover to check on it before 3 hours. Some butter may pool on top and will mix back in with the pasta when you are ready to serve.

Crustless Bacon and Broccoli Quiche

- 1 1/2 C. broccoli, chopped and cooked, not soggy
- 2 C. Swiss cheese, shredded
- 4 GF bacon strips, cooked
- 8 eggs, whisked
- 2 C. heavy cream
- 1 tsp. sea salt
- 1/4 tsp. black pepper

Preheat oven to 350°. Grease a 9 inch pie plate with spray or butter. Toss together bacon and broccoli. Add cheese. Mix all wet ingredients by hand. Add seasonings. Mix everything together and pour into pie plate. Bake uncovered for 45 minutes. Check to make sure the center is fully cooked. A knife put into the center will come out clean. The top will be light brown in color. Yield: 6 servings

Dutch Baby Breakfast Pancake
A Koprowski family Christmas favorite

- 1/4 C. unsalted butter
- 6 eggs, room temperature
- 1 C. milk
- 1 C. GF all purpose flour, see Two Flowers recipe
- 1/4 tsp xanthan gum
- 1/4 tsp. nutmeg
- 1 T. sugar
- 1/4 tsp. sea salt
- Garnish:
- Powdered sugar
- 1 T. fresh lemon juice

Preheat oven to 400°. Place butter in a 2 quart casserole dish and melt butter in oven. Coat bottom of the dish with melted butter. Blend eggs in a blender with milk. Add flour, sugar, gum and seasonings. Process until smooth. Pour batter into prepared casserole dish. Bake 15 to 20 minutes until edges are golden brown and the center starts to puff. Pancake will deflate when you take it out of oven. Dust with powdered sugar and drizzle with lemon juice. Also good topped with fresh berries. Serve immediately.

Fennel-Crusted Pork Loin with Roasted Vegetables and Pears

Kara Koprowski

- 1 T. fennel seeds
- 2 garlic cloves, minced
- 4 T. olive oil
- Coarse sea or Kosher salt and pepper
- 2 lb. boneless pork loin
- 2 red onions, peeled and quartered
- 1 pound small red or fingerling potatoes, halved or quartered
- 3 firm pears such as Bosc or Bartlett

Preheat oven to 400°. Using the bottom of a heavy pan, crush fennel seeds. Combine with garlic, 2 Tablespoons oil, 1 tsp. salt and 1/2 tsp. pepper. Rub mixture on all sides of the pork and place in large roasting pan. In a bowl, mix onions, potatoes and pears, 1 tsp, salt and 1 tsp. pepper and 2 Tablespoons olive oil. Scatter around pork and roast until pork is cooked through about 70 minutes. Internal temperature should be 170°. Transfer to cutting board, tent with foil and let pork rest at least 5 minutes before slicing. Serve with roasted vegetables and pears.

Flounder Piccata

- 4 oz. uncooked wild rice mixture, do not use the seasoning package if you are using a box
- 1/4 tsp. sea salt
- 1/8 tsp. white pepper
- 1 1/2 lbs. flounder fillets, thawed if using frozen
- 2 T. GF all purpose flour, see Two Flowers recipe
- 2 tsp. olive oil
- 1/2 C. white wine
- 2 T. fresh lemon juice plus extra slices for garnish
- 1 T. capers, drained
- 2 T. unsalted butter
- 4 C. fresh spinach

Cook rice according to package directions. Stir in salt and pepper. Sprinkle fish with an additional 1/4 teaspoon sea salt and 1/4 teaspoon pepper. Dredge fish in the flour. Heat oil in fry pan and cook fillets for 2 minutes on each side until fish flakes. To the pan add wine, juice, and capers. Cook 1 minute. Add butter to pan until it melts. In another pan, sauté spinach until it is wilted. To serve, place cooked rice on the bottom of a serving dish, next layer the spinach then the fish. Yield: 4 servings

Greek Shrimp Risotto

- 3 C. GF chicken broth see Two Flowers recipe
- 1 C. water
- 2 tsp. olive oil
- 3 C. onion, chopped
- 1 C. Arborio rice
- 2 garlic cloves, minced
- 1 3/4 C. sliced asparagus, cooked but crisp
- 1 lb. shrimp, cut into cubes, cooked
- 1/2 C. Feta cheese
- 1 T. dill, minced
- 2 T. lemon juice
- 1/4 tsp. black pepper

Bring broth and water to a simmer. Do not boil. Set aside. Heat oil and sauté chopped onion in a large skillet until tender. Add rice and garlic. Add broth mixture 1/2 cup at a time, stirring until all liquid is absorbed. This will take about 30 minutes. Stir in shrimp and asparagus. Remove from heat and stir in cheese and remaining ingredients. Yield: 6 cups

Green Tea Poached Fish
Kara Koprowski

Poaching Liquid:
- 5 C. water
- Knob of ginger, peeled and roughly chopped
- 2 T. sea salt
- 1 T. black peppercorns, whole
- 1 lime, cut in wheels
- 3 T. honey
- 1 C. prepared green tea, room temperature

- 4 6 to 8 oz. fish fillets, salmon works especially well but so do other types of white fish such as cod

Sauce:
- 1/3 C. prepared green tea
- 1 T. honey
- 1/2 lime, juiced and zested

Bring poaching liquid ingredients to a boil in a large saucepan. Reduce heat to medium and add fish fillets. Cover and poach 6 to 8 minutes, depending on thickness of fish fillets. Fish will flake with a fork when done. Prepare sauce while fish is cooking. Whisk together tea, honey, lime juice and zest from 1/2 lime in a small bowl. Spoon over poached fish. Yield: 4 to 6 servings

Ham & Aspargus Rice Bake

- 4 oz. wild rice, uncooked. Do not use seasoning if you are using a boxed item
- 1/2 C. brown or white rice, uncooked
- 1 1/2 lbs. fresh asparagus, cut into 1" pieces
- 2 C. GF ham, cubed, cooked
- 5 T. unsalted butter
- 12 eggs
- 1/2 C. milk
- 1 tsp. sea salt
- 1/4 tsp. pepper

Cheese Sauce:
- 2 T. canola oil
- 3 T. GF all purpose flour, see Two Flowers recipe
- 1 C. milk
- 2 C. Gouda cheese, shredded
- 1/2 tsp. ground ginger

Preheat oven to 325°. Cook all rice according to package directions and spread in greased 9 x 13 baking dish. Cook asparagus pieces in 1/2 inch of water, simmering about 5 minutes. Keep them crisp. Drain. Sauté ham in 2 tablespoons of butter. Spoon ham over rice. Heat remaining butter until hot. Whisk eggs, milk, salt and pepper in a small bowl. To remaining butter in a skillet, add the egg mixture and cook until eggs are set. Spoon over ham and top with asparagus. Sauce: Heat oil, stir in flour until smooth. Stir in milk and bring to a boil. Cook and stir for 2 minutes. Reduce heat and add cheese and ginger. Stir until a smooth sauce is formed. Pour over the casserole and bake at 325° for 30 minutes covered. Uncover and bake 10 to 15 minutes more. Yield: 10 servings

Mac & Cheese
A little richer but why not?

- 7 T. unsalted butter
- 4 T. soy flour
- 2 C. milk
- 2 T. cream cheese
- 1 tsp. sea salt
- 1/4 tsp. pepper
- 1 tsp. onion powder
- 1/4 tsp. dry mustard
- 1/8 tsp. nutmeg
- 1/4 tsp. paprika
- 2 C. sharp cheddar cheese, shredded
- 1 C. Gruyere cheese, shredded
- 1 lb. GF elbow macaroni, brown rice is a good one, cooked and drained. Leave some of the cooking water in the pot and return cooked pasta to the pot if it is ready before the cheese sauce. It is best to under cook the pasta by 1 or 2 minutes since it will be baking further in the oven.

Preheat oven to 350°. In a medium saucepan over medium heat, melt butter and mix in soy flour. Stir until it is a roux and very light tan in color. In the microwave or in another small pot on the stove, melt the cream cheese in milk over low heat. Slowly add the milk mixture to the flour and butter. Add seasonings. Stir in cheese. Mix the cheese sauce into the cooked macaroni. Stir carefully as the pasta tends to break. Put into a buttered casserole dish and bake at 350° for 45 minutes uncovered. If top gets too brown cover with foil. Yield 6 to 8 servings

Pad Thai

This is a vegan version of Pad Thai but protein can easily be added

- 16 oz. thick rice noodles
- 8 T. peanut butter or a nut butter of choice
- 2/3 C. GF soy sauce
- 2/3 C. orange juice
- 4 T. GF chili sauce, see Two Flowers recipe
- 1 T. red pepper flakes
- 1/2 C. onion, chopped
- 2 garlic cloves, minced
- 4 T. peanut oil
- 4 C. bean sprouts
- 1/2 C. green onions, white bulbs and tops, cut on a slant
- 2 tsp. fresh ginger, peeled and grated
- 2 T. cashews, halves
- 2 T. GF peanuts, not dry roasted
- 1 T. paprika
- 1/2 tsp. orange zest
- Sliced oranges and limes for garnish

Prepare rice noodles according to the package directions. Drain and set aside. In a large skillet over medium heat, combine nut butter, soy, orange juice, chili sauce, and pepper flakes. Heat until combined and bubbling, 2 to 3 minutes. Pour out of skillet into a bowl and set mixture aside. Using the same skillet, heat peanut oil and sauté the onions and garlic, stirring constantly over medium heat until onion is translucent. Pour in reserved liquid mixture and stir well. Add the cooked rice noodles. Add bean sprouts, green onions, ginger, nuts, paprika and zest. Stir over low heat until combined. Garnish with sliced limes and oranges. Note: You can add 1-2 cups of cooked chicken, shrimp or sautéed firm tofu to change this dish from vegetarian. Add cooked protein to dish when adding the rice noodles. Yield 6 to 8 servings.

Potato Crusted Quiche

24 oz. hash brown potatoes, thawed, Oreida is GF
1/3 C. unsalted butter, melted
1 C. Swiss cheese, shredded
1 C. jack cheese, shredded
1 C. GF ham, diced
1/2 C. cream or milk
3 large eggs, beaten
1/2 tsp. sea salt

Preheat oven to 425°. Grease a 9 inch pie plate. Press the thawed hash brown potatoes between paper towels to remove water. Press the hash browns into the pie plate and up the sides to form a crust. Brush the crust with the melted butter. Bake for 25 minutes in a 425° oven. Remove the pie pan and spread the cheeses and ham over the crust. Whisk the eggs, cream and seasonings together and pour over the baked crust. Bake uncovered at 350° for 30 to 40 minutes or until filling is firm and top is golden. Yield: 8 servings

Pretzel Chicken

1/2 lb. GF pretzels
1/2 C. canola oil
1/2 C. whole grain mustard
2 T. Dijon mustard
1/4 C. white wine
3 T. red wine vinegar
1 1/2 lbs. chicken breasts
1/4 tsp. sea salt
1/4 tsp. pepper

Preheat oven to 400°. Process pretzels until they are coarsely ground. Remove from processor. In clean processor add oil, mustards, vinegars and seasonings to make a dressing. Toss the chicken breasts in 1/2 of the dressing and then roll into pretzels. Bake at 400° for 20 to 25 minutes, uncovered. Slice chicken and serve with the remaining mustard dressing.

Quinoa Stuffed Peppers

1/2 C. quinoa
1 C. chicken broth, see Two Flowers recipe
6 bell peppers, different colors
1 T. olive oil
2 minced garlic cloves
1/4 C. sweet onion, chopped
1 small zucchini, chopped

1 lb. ground beef or ground turkey
2 T. GF Worcestershire sauce
1/4 tsp. sea salt
1/2 tsp. pepper
2 C. fresh tomatoes, chopped
1 T. basil, chopped
1/2 C. mozzarella cheese, shredded

Preheat oven to 350°. Cook quinoa in chicken broth for 15 minutes until liquid is absorbed. Cut tops off peppers and clean out the insides. Chop the tops. Heat oil and brown onion, garlic and seasoning. Add pepper tops, zucchini and cook to soften. Add meat, Worcestershire sauce, salt and pepper and brown the mixture. Add tomatoes and basil. Stir in quinoa and half the cheese. Stuff the peppers and top each pepper with the other half of the cheese. Bake at 350° uncovered, for 30 minutes until filling is hot. Yield: 5 to 6 servings

Retro Pot Roast
Old-fashioned pot roast but still in fashion

- 4 lbs. blade cut chuck roast, bone-in
- 1/3 C. GF all purpose flour, see Two Flowers recipe
- 1 tsp. pure paprika
- 1/4 tsp. sea salt
- 1/4 tsp. black pepper
- 2 T. canola oil
- 1 C. sweet onion, chopped, or 2 C. pearl onions, fresh or frozen thawed
- 4 slices GF bacon, chopped
- 2 bay leaves
- 2 C. fresh tomatoes, diced and seeded
- 2 ribs of celery, whole
- 5 carrots, whole peeled
- 3 turnips, optional
- 2 lbs. fingerling potatoes, whole, not peeled
- 1 T. red wine to taste, to add to gravy
- 2 C. GF beef broth, see Two Flowers recipe

Thickening:
- 1 T. GF all purpose flour, see Two flowers recipe
- 1/4 C. red wine or water

Preheat oven to 325°. Mix the flour and seasonings and coat all sides of the chuck roast. In a roasting pan with a lid, heat the oil. Add roast and brown until meat forms a brown crust. Add onions and bacon. Cook until onions are golden brown and bacon is crisp. Add tomatoes, bay leaves and beef broth. Roast meat, covered for 1 1/2 hours then add vegetables and potatoes. Return to oven and roast an additional 1 1/2 hours more until the meat reaches 185° internal temperature. Add a little beef broth or red wine if roast starts to dry out. Remove roast from the oven. Remove the sauce that has collected in the bottom of the pan and add it to the skillet to make the gravy. Add GF flour and wine or water to pan juices and cook over medium heat until thick, stirring constantly. This will be extra gravy for your roast and vegetables. Cool at least 5 minutes before slicing. Yield: 6 servings

Salmon with Ginger Soy Sauce

2 T. GF all purpose flour, see Two Flowers recipe
1 T. cornstarch
1 lb. salmon fillets, wild not farmed
1 T. canola oil
1/3 C. apple juice, unsweetened
2 C. green onions, chopped
2 tsp. ginger, minced
3 T. GF soy sauce
2 T. honey
1 T. balsamic vinegar
1/2 tsp. garlic, minced

Preheat oven to 200°. Combine flour and cornstarch. Dip fillets in mixture. Coat bottom of frying pan with canola oil and fry fillets about 6 minutes. Fish must flake apart with a fork. Remove fish and keep warm in a 200° oven. Add apple juice to pan and stir up the bits from the bottom of the pan. Stir in the remaining ingredients and blend sauce for 2 minutes. Spoon over salmon for serving. Yield: 4 servings

Salmon, Roasted in the Oven with Tangerine Relish

2 lbs. center cut salmon fillet with the skin on the bottom, wild salmon, not farmed
2 tsp. olive oil
1/2 tsp. salt
1/4 tsp. pepper
Relish:
1 C. tangerine segments, cut into small pieces
1/2 C. scallions, sliced
1 1/2 tsp. fresh ginger, sliced
2 tsp. fresh lemon juice
2 tsp. olive oil
1/2 tsp. salt
1/4 tsp. pepper

Preheat oven to 500°. Put a cookie sheet in the oven to heat it up. Cut salmon into 4 pieces, cleaning any white fat from the fillets. Leave the skin intact on the bottom of the fillets. Pat salmon dry with a paper towel. Brush the fillets with oil and sprinkle with salt and pepper. Reduce heat to 275° and remove the hot cookie sheet. Place fillets on the cookie sheet, skin side down. Roast to 125° internal temperature, about 15 minutes, depending on the thickness of the salmon. Yield: 4 servings
Relish:
Strain the tangerines over a bowl for about 15 minutes. Pour off juice but save 1 tablespoon. Into the juice whisk the lemon juice, ginger, scallions and oil. Stir in the tangerine pieces. Top the warm salmon with the relish.

Sausage Breakfast Patties
No effort to make your own

1/4 C. water
1 tsp. sea salt
2 tsp. sage
1 tsp. pepper

1/2 tsp. nutmeg
1/4 tsp. red pepper flakes
1/8 tsp. ground ginger
2 lbs. ground pork

Combine water and seasonings. Add pork and mix well. With your hands shape mixture into 4 inch patties. The patties will need to cook for 6 minutes on each side. They must be cooked through until the center is no longer pink. Yield: 8 or more patties

Southwestern Lasagna

4 T. canola oil
1 C. onion, finely chopped
2 lb. ground beef, pork or chicken
2 T. GF taco seasoning, see Two Flowers recipe
4 C. tomato salsa, see Two Flowers recipe
16 corn tortillas cut in quarters
2 1/2 C. frozen peas, thawed
4 C. cheddar cheese, shredded
1 C. mild chilies, chopped
2 C. sour cream
1/2 C. cilantro, chopped

Homemade re-fried beans:
2 C. pinto beans, cooked
1/2 C. onion, chopped
1 T. bacon fat or olive oil
1/4 C. water for thinning

Preheat oven to 400°. See Two Flowers recipe for cooking dried beans. Sauté the 1/2 cup of onion for the beans. Drain the beans and add the onions and start to mash them with a potato masher. Add water if beans are too thick. Set aside and reserve 2 cups for this recipe. Heat oil, sauté onion until soft. Add beef and cook. Mix seasoning with 1/2 cup water and add to meat mixture and stir until it is saucy. Lightly grease a 9 x 13 casserole dish. Cover the bottom of casserole with 1/3 of the salsa. Place the tortillas on the bottom of casserole to cover completely, piecing when necessary. Top with half the meat and half the peas. Sprinkle with 2/3 cup cheese. Cover with another layer of tortillas. Spread 1 cup salsa and the re-fried beans. Sprinkle with chilies and cheese. Layer with remaining tortillas, meat and peas. Sprinkle with 1/2 the remaining cheese. Cover and bake for 25 minutes at 400°. Uncover and sprinkle the remaining cheese on top and bake until bubbly about 10 more minutes. Let sit for 10 minutes. This will let the casserole settle. Top with sour cream and cilantro. Yield: 8 servings

Spaghetti Squash "Noodles" with Sauteed Vegetable Sauce

- 2 lb. spaghetti squash
- 1 T. olive oil
- 1 C. sweet onion, chopped
- 1 1/2 C. zucchini, chopped
- 3 C. Swiss chard, slivered
- 1/2 C. roasted red peppers, chopped
- 1/2 C. portobello mushrooms, chopped
- 4 garlic cloves, minced
- 2 C. Roma tomatoes, chopped
- 1 T. capers, drained
- 1/4 C. fresh parsley, chopped
- 2 T. fresh basil, chopped
- 1/4 C. red wine vinegar
- 1/2 C. Parmesan cheese, slivered, not granular
- 1/4 tsp. pepper
- 1/2 tsp. sea salt

Preheat oven to 400°. Place the whole squash on the rack of the oven and bake for at least an hour. It will be soft to the touch. After it is baked, let it cool. Cut it in half. Scoop out all the noodles and put them in a bowl. In a skillet heat the olive oil. Add the onions, garlic, zucchini and Swiss chard. Sauté for 10 minutes. Add the peppers, tomatoes, and mushrooms. Add the rest of the ingredients except the cheese and cook for a few minutes. Toss the vegetable mixture with the squash. Sprinkle the cheese on top. If necessary add more salt and pepper. Yield: 6 entree servings

Spinach Polenta Torte
Makes a good breakfast pie

5 C. water	1 10 oz. frozen spinach, chopped
1 1/2 C. cornmeal	1 10 oz. frozen kale, chopped
1/2 tsp. salt	2 T. olive oil
1/4 tsp. pepper	1/4 C. sweet onion, diced
1/2 C. Parmesan cheese, grated	2 garlic cloves, minced1
1/2 C. mozzarella cheese,	4 oz. GF bacon, uncooked and shredded sliced

Preheat oven to 400°. Thaw out the greens and squeeze out any excess water. They should be dry. In a skillet cook the bacon. Drain on paper towels. Sauté both greens with the olive oil, onion, and garlic. Add the seasonings. Mix the greens with the cooked bacon. Butter an 8 inch springform pan or an 8 inch pie plate. If you are using a springform pan line it with foil or parchment paper to keep the juices from dripping out. You can also use a 2 quart casserole dish. Bring 4 cups of water to a boil, reserving 1 cup. Stir the cornmeal salt and pepper into a bowl. Add the reserved water to the cornmeal and stir well. Pour the cornmeal mixture into the boiling water a little at a time. Stir constantly until cooked, about 10 min- utes. Divide the polenta into thirds. Line the bottom of the prepared pan with 1/3rd. of the polenta. Add half the spinach/kale mixture into the next layer and half the cheeses. Reserve 1/2 cup of moz- zarella for the top. Repeat with another layer of polenta and use the rest of the greens and cheese as the next layer. Top with the remaining polenta. Sprinkle the reserved 1/2 cup mozzarella over the top. Bake for 30 minutes in a 400° oven loosely covered with foil. Yield: 6 to 8 servings.

Swedish Meatballs

Still not sure how the Polish mother-in-law knew how to cook a Swedish recipe

Meat Mixture:
1 lb. ground chuck
1 lb. ground pork
1 lb. ground veal
3/4 C. whipping cream
1 1/2 C. almond flour
1 1/2 C. onion, minced
3 egg yolks
1/2 tsp. nutmeg
1/2 tsp. allspice
1/4 tsp. black pepper
6 T. unsalted butter
Sauce:
3 T. unsalted butter
6 T. brown rice flour
1 1/2 C. GF beef broth, see Two Flowers recipe
1 1/2 tsp. sugar
4 oz. cream cheese
1 bay leaf
1 lb. GF noodles, see Two Flower recipe, or rice

Preheat oven to 350°. Break up the raw meat with a fork and mix well. Sauté onions in 2 tablespoons butter. Add almond meal and stir as it lightly toasts. Set aside. Add seasonings to the raw meat and mix in the egg yolks. Add the onion/almond mixture and mix well with your hands. Form 1 to 2 inch balls. Sauté the meatballs in the rest of the butter on top of the stove turning them frequently. It should take about 10 minutes to cook them off. Meanwhile make the sauce. Melt butter and add brown rice flour. Stir until it thickens and let the flour brown a little. Melt cream cheese into sauce. Add sugar, bay leaf and beef broth. Continue to cook as it thickens. Remove from heat. Put meatballs in a casserole and cover with sauce. Bake in a 350° oven, covered for about 10 to 15 minutes. Serve over GF noodles or rice. Yield: 8 servings

Tilapia Tacos
Ken Koprowski's The Fat Taco

2 slices purple onion slices
1 C. bell peppers, any color, slivered
1 avocado, sliced
1/8 C. cilantro
1 jalapeno pepper, thinly slivered
2 tsp. canola oil
1 tsp. sea salt
1/2 tsp. black pepper
1/2 C. cherry tomatoes, cut in half
8 corn tortillas
8 wedges of lime

4 5 oz. tilapia fillets, not farm raised. You can use any white fish.

Preheat oven to 200°. Grill onion slices and bell peppers. Cut the onion slices in half and set aside. Sauté tilapia in oil and fry 3 minutes on each side. Salt and pepper the fillets. Flake fish into bite sized pieces. Warm the corn tortillas in a 200° oven to soften. Divide the fish and onion mixture between the 8 tortillas. Add the avocado, cilantro, and cherry tomatoes to each taco. Serve with the lime wedge to juice the top. Yield: 8 fish tacos.

Tortilla Bake

18 oz. GF Sausage, browned, all fat drained
3/8 C. chunky salsa, see Two Flowers recipe
12 corn tortillas
3 C. cheddar, shredded
3/8 C. green onions, sliced
2 1/4 C. milk
8 eggs
3/8 tsp. chili powder
3/8 tsp. ground cumin
Toppings:
Salsa
Sour cream
Black olives
Shredded jack cheese

Preheat oven to 350°. Mix sausage and salsa in a small bowl. In the bottom of a greased 10 inch round pie pan or casserole dish, put 6 corn tortillas flat on the bottom. Sprinkle with 1/2 of the browned sausage mixture. Sprinkle 1/2 of the cheese and 1/2 of the onions, over the meat layer. Layer the remaining tortillas, sausage, cheese and green onions in the pan. Mix eggs, milk, chili powder and cumin in a bowl. Whisk and pour mixture over the stack. Bake at 350° for 35 to 40 minutes until an inserted knife comes out clean. Cut into wedges. Serve toppings on the side. Yield: 6 servings

Vegetarian Chili, Oven Roasted

- 2 1/2 C. dry mixed beans, kidney, white, black are a good mix
- 1/4 C. chili powder
- 1/2 tsp. sea salt
- 1 jalapeno chili, crushed
- 1/4 C. shitake mushrooms, minced
- 4 tsp. dried oregano
- 1 T. cumin
- 1/2 C. walnuts or other nuts of choice, toasted
- 4 C. tomatoes, chopped
- 3 T. tomato paste
- 6 garlic cloves, minced
- 1/4 C. cilantro, chopped
- 1 T. ground cumin
- 2 T. GF soy sauce
- 1/4 C. canola oil
- 7 C. water
- 4 C. onions, chopped
- 1 C. carrots, shredded or minced
- 1/2 C. red pepper, diced

Toppings:
- 1/2 avocado, chopped
- 1/2 C. sharp cheddar, shredded
- 1/2 C. sour cream or yogurt

Preheat oven to 300°. Rinse beans and cook in a saucepan with 4 quarts of water. Bring to a boil. Remove from heat, cover and let stand for 1 hour. Drain and rinse the beans. Process toasted nuts to a fine grind. Set aside. Process tomatoes, tomato paste, jalapeno, garlic, dry seasonings and soy sauce, until a coarse mixture is reached. Set aside. Heat the oil on the stove and cook down the remaining vegetables until onions start to brown. Drain off the liquid and reserve for thinning if necessary. Add the rinsed beans and 7 cups of water to to the vegetables. Bring to a boil. Put the vegetable/bean mixture into a roasting pan and bake in a 300° oven, covered for 45 minutes. Remove from oven and add the tomato mixture, walnuts, and the reserved liquid. Bake for another 2 hours until the beans are soft. If your mixture is too thick puree more tomatoes to turn them to juice for thinning. Stir in the parsley. Let chili stand uncovered for 20 minutes. Serve with toppings of choice. Yield: 6 servings

Vegetable Quiche Cups
Kara Koprowski

- 6 eggs, well beaten
- 2 C. fresh spinach, steamed and well drained
- 1 C. cheddar cheese, shredded
- 1/4 C. red bell peppers, diced, can use fresh or roasted
- 1/4 C. onion, diced
- 1/4 C. fresh goat cheese, crumbled
- 5 drops hot pepper sauce, such as Sriracha
- Pinch of salt and pepper
- Optional: 1/4 C. salsa, see Two Flowers recipe

Preheat oven to 350°. Line a 12 cup muffin pan with paper muffin cups. Spray muffin cups with cooking spray. Combine eggs, cheddar cheese, spinach, peppers, onions, hot pepper sauce, salt and pepper. Divide batter evenly among muffin cups. Sprinkle crumbled goat cheese in center of each muffin cup. Bake at 350° for 20 minutes until muffins are puffed and golden brown. Cool for 5 minutes on wire rack. Cups can be frozen and reheated in the microwave. You can use a variety of grilled or steamed vegetables in this recipe. You can also spoon a scant teaspoon of salsa in the center of each cup before baking for some added zing. Yield: 12 muffins

Veggie Burgers

- 2 T. olive oil
- 4 garlic cloves, minced
- 3 T. sweet onions, minced
- 3 T. red or green bell peppers, minced
- 3 T. carrots, grated
- 1 C. garbanzo beans, cooked
- 1 C. black beans, cooked
- 2 eggs, beaten
- 2 tsp. cumin
- 2 tsp. paprika
- 1 tsp. chili powder
- 3/4 C. quinoa, cooked
- 2 C. fresh spinach, finely slivered, stems removed

See Two Flowers recipe for cooking dried beans. In olive oil, sauté onions, peppers, carrots, garlic until softened. In a separate bowl, mix eggs with spices and quinoa. Add vegetables and spinach and mix gently. Divide mixture into 4 patties. Place patties on a baking sheet and refrigerate the "meat" mixture overnight before frying in canola or vegetable oil. You can also bake patties in a 375° oven for approximately 10 minutes. I find that baked burgers are easier to handle. Yield: 4 to 6 patties

White Autumn Vegetable Lasagna

- 4 T. unsalted butter
- 4 1/2 C. peeled, cubed butternut squash, cooked
- 4 C. GF white sauce, see Two Flowers recipe
- 2 cans pure pumpkin puree, not pie filling
- 3 plum tomatoes, sliced
- 2 eggs
- 20 rice flour wrappers
- 1 lb. Gouda cheese, shredded
- 16 basil leaves, chopped

Preheat oven to 400°. Cook the squash in water before peeling it, for 15 minutes. Peel and cube. Toss the butter with cooked squash and lightly mix. Make 4 cups of gluten free white sauce. Set aside. Soak rice wrappers in hot water to soften as you use each one. Grease a 9 x 13 casserole. Spread 1 cup of white sauce on the bottom of casserole. Mix eggs with pumpkin. Spread 1 cup of pumpkin mixture on top of the wrappers. Sprinkle with 2/3 cup of cheese. Put on one more layer of wrappers. Spread 1 cup of white sauce and top with squash, basil, and half of the remaining cheese. The last layer will end with wrappers, tomatoes slices and remaining cheese. Bake covered for 30 minutes at 400°. Uncover and add remaining cheese to the top and bake for 10 minutes more. Yield: 8 servings

Sauces & Dressings

Alfredo Sauce

8 oz. cream cheese, softened
1 C. milk
1 C. heavy cream
1/4 C. unsalted butter

3/4 C. Parmesan cheese
1 garlic clove, minced
1/4 C. minced parsley

In a saucepan heat cream, butter and milk. Add cream cheese and stir until it is melted. It will now be hot and thickened. Stir in garlic and Parmesan cheese. Stir in parsley. Yield: about 4 cups

Apple and Sage Sauce for Pork

2 T. canola oil
1 C. sweet onion, chopped
15 apple wedges, sprinkled with sea salt
1 C. pure apple cider, not juice
6 T. apple brandy
1 1//2 C. GF chicken broth, see Two Flowers recipe

4 T. sage, minced
6 T. cream cheese for thickening
4 tsp. cider vinegar
1/4 tsp. pepper

Sauté onion and apple in oil until tender. In the pan that you roasted a pork roast, add the softened onion/apple mixture and scrape up the pork bits. Stir in all the liquid ingredients. Simmer the mixture until it cooks down to a thicker sauce. The liquid will be absorbed. Stir in the cream cheese and sage. Spoon over the pork. Yield: This sauce will cover about four pounds of pork

Apricot or Blackberry Glaze
Glaze for chicken or fish on the grill

3/4 C. preserves, apricot or blackberry
1/4 tsp. whole grain GF mustard
3 T. GF Dijon mustard

4 T. unsalted butter, melted
2 T. shallots, coarsely chopped
1/2 tsp. sea salt
3 T. water

Process all ingredients in food processor until combined. Reserve 1/2 of the glaze for serving. Use the other half to brush on chicken or fish for grilling. Yield 1 1/2 cups of glaze

Avocado Vinaigrette
Kara Koprowski

- 2 ripe avocados
- 4 T. olive oil
- 3 T. fresh cilantro, chopped, stems discarded
- 1/4 C. red onion, chopped
- 1 small fresh jalapeno, diced, seeded with membrane discarded
- 3 to 4 T. water
- 1/4 C. red wine vinegar
- fresh lime juice from 1/2 squeezed fresh lime
- 2 garlic cloves, chopped
- Big pinch sea salt and fresh ground black pepper

Peel & chop avacodos. Puree all ingredients in a blender until smooth. Add more lime juice if dressing needs more zing. Great over simple greens as well as on roasted vegetables and in tacos. Keep tightly covered in refrigerator, since it contains fresh avocados. Use within 2 hours.

Basic White Sauce
Can be turned into a cheese sauce

- 1/4 C. unsalted butter, cut in cubes
- 1T. tapioca flour
- 1T. rice flour
- 1T. sorghum flour
- 2 C. whole milk
- 8 oz. cream cheese
- 1/2 tsp. salt
- 1/2 tsp. pepper
- For Cheese Sauce:
- 2 C. sharp cheddar cheese, shredded
- 2 T. GF Dijon mustard

In a saucepan, melt butter and whisk in the flour. Slowly add milk, flour and butter mixture. Whisk until thickened and hot. Add salt and pepper. Do not boil. Add the cheddar cheese and Dijon mustard if you want to make a cheese sauce. Yield about 2 cups

Basil Pesto
Tish's Traditional pesto

2 T. red wine vinegar
1/4 C. basil leaves, tightly packed
3 T. parsley
1 garlic clove, minced

1/2 tsp salt
1/2 tsp. sugar
1/4 C. Parmesan cheese, grated
1/3 C. olive oil
1 T. pine nuts, toasted

Combine all ingredients in a blender or food processor, pulsing to combine. Keep slightly chunky. Let stand at room temperature before using so the flavors can blend. Store in refrigerator in a glass container. Freezes well.

B.B.Q. Sauce

1/2 C. olive Oil
5 garlic cloves, minced
1 C. sweet onion, chopped
1 C. fresh tomatoes, seeded and chopped

2 T. GF soy sauce
1 C. orange juice
1/4 C. brown sugar
2 T. cider vinegar
1/2 C. fresh parsley, chopped

Heat olive oil and add garlic and onions and sauté until soft. Add tomatoes and cook until reduced to half of original volume. Stir in the remaining ingredients and cook 20 minutes more. Yield: 2 Cups

Berry Jam

5 C. fresh berries
2 C. sugar

2 C. honey
1/4 C. lemon juice

Mix all ingredients and bring to a boil in a saucepan. Cook uncovered until mixture reaches 220°. For seedless jam, press through a strainer. Pour into jars with lids in usable portions. Use within 2 weeks. Store extra jam in freezer.

Berry Sauce

- 2 C. of either: blueberries, blackberries, raspberries, strawberries. You can also mix two of them
- 1/2 C. water
- 3/4 C. sugar
- 1 C. orange juice
- 1 tsp. orange peel, grated
- 1 tsp. GF pure vanilla
- 3 T. cornstarch
- 1/8 tsp. cinnamon
- 1/8 tsp. nutmeg

In a saucepan mix 1/4 cup water, sugar, juice, orange peel, and berry choice. Mix cornstarch with 1/4 cup cornstarch and stir until dissolved. Pour into berry mix and simmer until mix starts to thicken. Stir but do not smash the berries! If too thick, thin with a little water. When thickened stir in spices and extracts. Yield: 3 1/2 cups

Berry Salsa

- 2 C. fresh blueberries
- 2 C. fresh strawberries
- 2 C. blackberries
- 1/8 C. sugar, may need more if berries are not ripe enough
- 2 T. chopped sweet onions
- 1 T. lemon juice
- 1 tsp. lemon zest
- 1/2 tsp. pepper
- 2 drops GF hot pepper sauce
- 1/2 C. toasted almonds, slivered

Mix all ingredients in a bowl except the almonds. You need to let this mixture sit in a refrigerator for at least an hour before serving. Right before serving stir in the almonds. Good with pork, chicken or fish. Yield: 6 cups

Blue Cheese Dressing

- 1 C. GF mayonnaise, see Two Flowers recipe
- 2 T. onion, finely chopped
- 1 tsp. garlic, minced
- 1/4 C. parsley, chopped
- 1/2 C. sour cream or buttermilk
- 1 T. lemon juice
- 1 T. white vinegar
- 1/4 C. blue cheese, crumbled
- 1/4 tsp. sea salt
- 1/8 tsp. fresh ground black pepper

Combine all ingredients with a whisk. Chill at least one hour or longer before use. Yield: about 1 1/2 cups

Broccoli Cream Sauce
Good over pasta, potatoes, or rice

2 C. broccoli florets
2 T. sweet onion, diced
2 C. whole milk
1/4 tsp. sea salt
1/8 tsp. white pepper

3 T. Parmesan cheese, grated
1 T. cornstarch
2 T. cold water
1 tsp. fresh basil, chopped

Steam broccoli until it is still crisp and not soggy. Drain. Sauté onions in a few tablespoons of olive oil until browned. Dissolve cornstarch in cold water. Stir in milk, Parmesan cheese and seasonings. Cook until it thickens. Add sauce to broccoli and cooked onion. Yield: about 5 cups

Butterscotch Sauce

2 T. unsalted butter
1/2 C. light brown sugar, packed
2/3 C. heavy cream or milk
1/4 tsp. GF pure vanilla

1/2 tsp. sea salt
Optional addition:
2 T. Dark rum
1/4 cup pecans

Melt butter in a saucepan. Add brown sugar and cook for 3 to 5 minutes. Add milk all at once. Cook 10 minutes more until the mixture becomes creamy. Yield: 1 cup

Caramelized Pineapple
Nice addition to pork or chicken

1 T. canola oil
1 1/2 tsp. sweet onion, minced
1 garlic clove, minced
2 C. fresh pineapple, diced
1 T. GF soy sauce

1 1/2 tsp. lime juice
1 tsp. ginger root, minced, peeled, not powdered
1 tsp. cilantro, chopped

Cook onion and garlic in oil for 2 minutes. Add fresh pineapple and cook for 5 minutes more until lightly browned. Add all other ingredients except cilantro and cook 2 minutes more. Remove from heat and cool. Stir in cilantro. Yield 2 cups

Chocolate Peanut Butter Sauce

1 T. unsalted butter
2 T. light brown sugar
1/4 C. chunky peanut butter
1/2 C. heavy cream
3/4 C. dark chocolate, chopped

Melt butter in a saucepan. Add sugar and whisk in peanut butter and cream. Bring to a boil and add chocolate. Whisk until dissolved. Store in refrigerator. Reheat in microwave to serve. Yield 2 cups

Chocolate Sauce

1/2 C. whole milk or cream
3 T. sugar
1 T. cocoa
1/4 C. semisweet chocolate chips
1/2 tsp. GF pure vanilla
Sprinkle of sea salt

Mix all ingredients together in a saucepan. Bring all ingredients to a boil, stirring constantly until thickened. Remove from heat and stir in vanilla. Yield: 3/4 cup of sauce

Citrus Herb Sauce
Use on chicken or fish

1 tsp. sea salt
1 tsp. pepper
1/2 tsp. paprika
4 T. unsalted butter
4 garlic cloves, minced
8 T. sweet sherry
4 T. lemon juice
2 tsp. lemon zest
1/2 tsp. fresh oregano, minced
1 T. fresh tarragon, minced
2 T. parsley, minced
1 T. fresh chives, chopped
1/2 tsp. rice flour

Sauté garlic in butter and stir until tender. Stir in sherry and lemon juice. Cook until liquid is almost evaporated. Stir in remaining ingredients. If you need thicker sauce whisk in rice flour before you add the herbs. Yield: enough for 2 pounds of chicken or fish.

Citrus Herb Stir Fry or Dipping Sauce
Kara Koprowski

1/4 C. low sodium GF soy sauce
3 T. fresh lemon juice
1 garlic clove, minced
1 T. sugar
2 T. fresh basil, chopped
2 T. fresh cilantro, chopped

In a small glass bowl, combine first four ingredients and stir until sugar is dissolved. Add fresh herbs. Can substitute orange juice for the lemon juice for a sweeter sauce. Can substitute mint for the cilantro or use all three herbs. Great in a stir fry instead of bottled sauce or use as a dipping sauce for chicken fingers. Yield: 1/2 cup

Coconut Curry Stir Fry Sauce
Kara Koprowski

1 1/2 C. canned light coconut milk
2 T. GF soy sauce
2 tsp. sugar
1/2 tsp. sea salt
2 T. olive oil
1 tsp. crushed red pepper flakes
Grated zest from one medium sized lemon
2 garlic cloves, minced
1 1/2 T. curry powder
1/2 C. fresh basil, chopped

In small bowl, combine coconut milk, soy sauce, sugar and salt. Stir until sugar dissolves. In a small wok or frying pan, heat olive oil over medium heat for 30 seconds. Add red pepper flakes, lemon zest, garlic cloves and curry powder. Stir fry mixture until fragrant about 30 seconds. Add coconut milk mixture and bring to a boil. Cook until sauce thickens about 2 minutes. Add basil and stir to combine. Yield: about 1 1/2 cups

Creamy Tomato Sauce

- 3 T. unsalted butter
- 2 T. prosciutto, minced
- 3/4 C. onions, minced
- 1 bay leaf
- Pinch of red pepper flakes
- 1 tsp. salt
- 3 garlic cloves, minced
- 2 T. tomato paste
- 1/4 C. sun-dried tomatoes, packed in oil, rinsed and chopped
- 1/4 C. white wine
- 2 C. fresh tomatoes, crushed
- 1/2 C. whipping cream
- 1/4 C. fresh basil, chopped

Melt butter in saucepan. Add prosciutto, onion, bay leaf and seasoning. Cook until onion is soft. Add garlic and cook until garlic starts to turn brown. Stir in paste, chopped sun-dried tomatoes and fresh tomatoes. Add wine and cook until liquid is evaporated. Cook sauce until it thickens. Add cream right before serving over pasta. Yield: 4 cups

Cutting Board Salsa
Kara Koprowski

- 2 C. plum tomatoes, diced
- 1/2 C. jicama, peeled and diced
- 1/2 C. sweet yellow onion, diced
- 1/2 C. radishes, diced
- 1/2 C. cucumber, seeded and diced
- 1/4 C. fresh orange juice
- 2 T. mint, chopped
- 2 T. cilantro, chopped
- 3 T. fresh lime juice
- 1 small jalapeno pepper, seeded and diced
- 1/2 tsp. salt

Gently combine all ingredients in a glass bowl and toss. Cover and chill. It is easy to make if you have the bowl sitting next to the cutting board and add each ingredient as you finish chopping. You can use all lime juice instead of orange and lime juice for a more tart salsa. Yield: 4 1/2 cups of salsa

Dill Sauce

1 C. sour cream or Greek yogurt
1 1/2 T. GF Dijon mustard
3 T. white vinegar
3 T. brown sugar
3 T. fresh dill, chopped
2 T. fresh cucumber, grated

Mix all the prepared ingredients and store in the refrigerator. Great with fish or as a vegetable dip. Yield: 1 1/2 cups

Ginger Dressing
Nice dressing for Asian dishes and noodle salads

3 cloves garlic, minced
2 T. ginger root, shaved
3/4 C. olive oil
1/3 C. rice vinegar
1/2 C. GF soy sauce
3 T. honey
1/4 C. water

Combine all the ingredients in a jar with a lid. Shake and store in the same jar. Refrigerate. Yield: about 1 3/4 cups

Hoisin Sauce

1 C. GF soy sauce
1/2 C. creamy peanut butter
1/2 C. honey or molasses
2 tsp. GF hot sauce
1/2 tsp. garlic powder
1/8 tsp. black pepper
2 1/2 T. rice vinegar

In a medium sized bowl, whisk all ingredients to incorporate. Refrigerate and store in a glass jar. Yield: 2 cups

Hot Bacon Dressing

1 lb. GF bacon
4 T. GF all purpose flour, see Two Flowers recipe
3 C. red wine vinegar
1 1/2 C. water
1 C. sugar

Cook bacon and reserve drippings. Add flour to drippings and stir to make a paste. Add vinegar, water and sugar to the paste. Stir and cook down. Add 1/2 of the cooked bacon to the dressing for flavor. Keep the other half for the salad. Dressing should look like thin gravy. Reheat to serve. Yield: about 5 cups

Ketchup
An Easy Do!

4 cups tomato puree, freshly made
1/4 C. onion, chopped
1/2 C. cider vinegar
1/4 C. GF brown rice syrup, not all rice syrup is GF

1/4 tsp. each of the following:
Allspice
Mace
Ginger
Ground cloves
Cayenne pepper
Black pepper
1/2 tsp. dry mustard
Sea salt

Core about 24 tomatoes. I do not remove the skins as the food processor minces them so finely you never notice them. Put the tomatoes into the processor and puree until they are sandy in texture. Combine all ingredients in a crock pot with the tomato puree and cook on high for 2 1/2 hours. Process in food processor until smooth. Put back into crock pot for 1 hour on high heat uncovered so it will thicken. Store in covered container in the refrigerator. Can also freeze. Yield: 4 cups

Marsala Mushroom Sauce

- 2 tsp. olive oil
- 2 T. unsalted butter
- 1/2 C. sweet onion, chopped
- 1/2 tsp. Herbs de Provence, see Two Flowers recipe
- 1/4 tsp. pepper
- 4 C. assorted fresh mushrooms, sliced
- 2 garlic cloves, minced
- 1 tsp. sea salt
- 1/4 C. Marsala wine or red wine, do not use cooking wine
- 2 C. GF beef broth, see Two Flowers recipe, for beef or pork
- 2 C. GF chicken broth, see Two Flowers recipe. for chicken
- 2 T. cornstarch

Use beef broth if you are cooking beef or pork. Use chicken broth for chicken or turkey. Dissolve cornstarch in 1/4 cup of your broth choice. Sauté mushrooms in 1 tablespoon of butter and 1 teaspoon of olive oil. Let them cook down to reduce liquid. The liquid will vary depending upon the type of mushroom you choose. Set the mushrooms aside. Sauté the onion and garlic in the remaining butter and olive oil until softened. Add seasonings and stir well. Add cooked mushrooms. Add broth and cornstarch to the mixture. Stir until it thickens, 3 to 5 minutes. At the end of the cooking time, add the Marsala or red wine. Yield: 3 to 4 cups

Mayonnaise
I don't think you will go back to the store shelf

- 1 1/2 C. high quality olive oil
- 1/2 C. canola oil
- 2 large egg + 2 egg yolks, use pasteurized eggs only
- 2 T. fresh lemon juice
- 1/4 tsp. sugar
- 1 tsp. sea salt, finely ground
- 1/2 tsp. white pepper
- 1/2 tsp. dry mustard

Mix the two oils together and put into a measuring cup. Put the eggs and the yolks into a food processor and blend. Slowly add the oil mixture in a steady stream into the egg mixture. It should take about 5 minutes. Blend in lemon juice and sugar. When completed add salt, pepper and dry mustard. Refrigerate in a glass container. Yield: 2+ cups

Peanut Butter

16 oz. fresh or plain peanuts, do not use dry roasted
1 tsp. sea salt
1 1/2 T. peanut oil
1 tsp. honey, optional

Place nuts and salt in food processor and start to process. Add peanut oil a little at a time until you are happy with the consistency. Add honey, if you are using honey. Store in a jar, unrefrigerated. Yield: 1 1/2 cups

Popsi's Favorite Applesauce
Gladys Nosse (Nana)

5 lbs. mixed apples, do not use Delicious or Golden Delicious apples
1/2 C. sugar or no sugar, it's up to you
Water as needed to thin
2 T. cinnamon
1/2 tsp. nutmeg, fresh grated is preferred

Core but do not peel apples. Cut apples in pieces. The smaller the pieces the quicker the sauce will cook down. Put apples into a large pot and fill with water about 1/4 the way up. Stir in sugar or not, as you wish. Keep stirring so it doesn't burn. Add water to thin as the apples cook down. When apples are fully cooked pick out the large peels. Puree the cooked apples in the food processor in batches. Do not fill processor more than 2/3 full. Add cinnamon and nutmeg. Freeze or store in refrigerator. Not sure of the yield because it will depend on your apples.

Ranch Dressing

1 C. buttermilk
1/2 C. GF mayonnaise, see Two Flowers recipe
1/2 C. sour cream
1/2 tsp. sea salt
1/2 tsp. onion powder
1/4 tsp. garlic powder
1 T. dried parsley
1/2 tsp. chives
1/2 tsp. thyme
1/2 tsp. cider vinegar
1/4 tsp. pepper

Whisk all ingredients together to mix well. Store in the refrigerator. Yield: 2 cups

Red Wine Vinaigrette

1/2 C. red wine vinegar	2 tsp. sea salt
1/4 C. fresh lemon juice	3/4 tsp. ground pepper
2 tsp. honey	1 C. olive oil

Place all ingredients, except olive oil, in a food processor. Blend. Slowly add oil to further process. Store in the refrigerator. Bring to room temperature before serving. Yield: about 2 cups

Roasted Tomato Sauce

Kara Koprowski. This is a flexible sauce.
Best part is there is no need to peel tomatoes.

10 to 15 plum tomatoes cut in half or 4 C. cherry or grape sized tomatoes	2 to 4 T. olive oil
	Splash of red wine vinegar
	Sea salt
4 garlic cloves, left whole, peeled	Pepper
	Sugar
1 sweet white or yellow onion, sliced	Parmesan cheese, grated

Preheat oven to 350°. Leave skins on tomatoes. Keep small tomatoes whole. Place tomatoes, garlic and onion in large glass baking dish. Drizzle with olive oil to coat tomatoes. You can add more after the tomatoes are done roasting. Sprinkle with sea salt and pepper. Roast at 350° for at least 30 minutes until skins begin to wrinkle and tomatoes have produced some juice. Skins may turn dark but you don't want them black since you are leaving skins on in the sauce. Remove from oven and cool to room temperature.

Puree everything including juices from the baking dish in a blender at low speed. With motor running, add a small stream of olive oil, a pinch of sugar, salt and pepper until sauce is a medium thick consistency. Can also add fresh herbs such as basil and oregano. A splash of red wine vinegar provides a brightness to the sauce. Store covered in refrigerator for up to a week or freeze. This sauce freezes nicely in quart sized Ziploc bags; frozen flat. Adjust salt and pepper to taste.

Variations: Can also add vegetables in addition to or or in place of some of the tomatoes such as carrots or bell peppers. Hard vegetables such as carrots may require a longer roasting time so cut in small pieces. Can add grated Parmesan cheese at end. Yield: Approximately 3 cups of sauce

Smashed Onion Jam
Kara Koprowski - great condiment to have on hand

18 to 20 shallots, peeled with root end removed
1 1/2 C. sugar
1 C. water
2 C. white wine vinegar
1/2 C. dry white wine
1 1/2 T. sea salt
3 to 4 sprigs fresh thyme

Cut shallots in half and place flat side down on a cutting board. Smash using the flat side of a large chef's knife, similar to how you smash garlic cloves. Combine sugar, water, vinegar, wine and salt in large saucepan over low heat. Stir to dissolve sugar. Add shallots, bay leaves and thyme. Raise heat to medium and bring to a boil. Reduce heat to a simmer and cook uncovered about an hour, stirring occasionally. Liquid will be reduced to a syrup. Remove from heat and cool. Keep covered in refrigerator for up to two weeks. Serve cold or at room temperature. Great condiment to use in sandwiches, over grilled meat, sausages, poultry or fish. Yield: About 5 cups

Stir Fry Sauce
Basic sauce ready for additions

2 T. peanut oil
2 T. sesame seeds
2 T. honey
2 tsp. fresh lemon juice
6 T. GF soy sauce
2 T. fresh ginger, peeled and minced
1 C. GF vegetable or GF chicken broth, see Two flowers recipe
6 T. cornstarch

Toast sesame seeds in the oil. Set aside. Dissolve cornstarch in the broth and stir until cornstarch is dissolved. In a wok or frying pan, cook honey, lemon juice, soy sauce, ginger and broth mixture over medium heat until thick about 2 minutes. Make this sauce first and add it to your finished stir fry. Your stir fry will have cooked more evenly without the sauce. Toss with toasted sesame seeds. Yield: 2 cups

Sweet Chili Sauce

1 T. fresh garlic, minced
1/2 C. honey
3 red chili peppers
3/4 C. water

1/2 C. GF white vinegar
1 T. salt
1 T. cornstarch
2 T. water

In the food processor chop up the chilies. I leave in the seeds for the spiciness. Put all the ingredients, except the cornstarch and the water in a sauce pan. Bring mixture to a boil. Add the cornstarch that has been dissolved in water to the hot mixture. Stir to incorporate. It will thicken slightly. Yield: 1 3/4 cups

Sweet Marinade
Jean Koprowski

1/2 C. water
1/2 C. sugar

1 C. cider vinegar
1 red onion, sliced

Mix all ingredients and store in the refrigerator. Great on cucumbers, cooked beets, cooked potatoes or green beans. Layer the vegetables with red onion slices and refrigerate several hours to blend the flavors. Keep turning the vegetables in the marinade. Yield: 1 1/2 cup. This amount will provide enough marinade for 4 cups of vegetables.

Sweet & Sour Sauce

2 T. cornstarch
1 C. pineapple juice
1/3 C. brown sugar
1 tsp. salt

1/2 C. pure GF ketsup, see Two Flowers recipe
1/4 C. cider vinegar
1/4 tsp. dry mustard

Dissolve cornstarch in pineapple juice in a saucepan. Add all other ingredients and stir until thicken. Cool. Store in refrigerator in a glass jar. Yield: 1 3/4 cups

Tartar Sauce

- 1 C. GF mayonnaise, see Two Flowers recipe
- 1/4 C. GF pickle relish
- 2 T. fresh parsley, chopped
- 2 tsp. onion, grated
- 1 T. fresh lemon juice
- 1/4 tsp. Worcestershire sauce

Whisk all ingredients together. Store in a jar in the refrigerator. Yield: 1 1/2 cups.

1,000 Island Dressing

- 1/2 C. sour cream
- 1/2 C. GF mayonnaise, see Two Flowers recipe
- 1/4 C. GF ketchup, see Two Flowers recipe
- 1 T. GF pickle relish
- 1/2 tsp. paprika
- 1 tsp. fresh lemon juice

Whisk all ingredients in a small bowl. Store in a glass jar and refrigerate. Yield: 1 1/4 cups

Tomato and Arugula Pesto
Kara Koprowski

- 1/4 C. pine nuts, toasted or almonds, slivered
- 2 1/2 C. cherry or grape tomatoes
- 1 C. arugula leaves, tightly packed
- 1 medium garlic clove, minced
- 1 tsp. table salt
- 1 tsp. black pepper
- Pinch red pepper flakes
- 1/3 C. olive oil
- 1 tsp. lemon zest, grated
- 1 T. lemon juice, fresh squeezed

Combine almonds, tomatoes, arugula, garlic, salt, pepper, red pepper flakes in food processor until smooth about 1 minute. Add lemon zest and juice. Scrape down sides with a spatula to make sure all ingredients are combined. With machine running, slowly drizzle in olive oil, about 30 seconds.

This recipe can be made in a blender. Pulse ingredients until roughly chopped and then add olive oil for approximately 15 seconds with blender running. This recipe will cover 1 pound of cooked GF pasta with 1/2 cup grated Parmesan cheese. Also excellent on top of grilled vegetables.

Tomato Pineapple Salsa

- 2 C. fresh tomatoes, seeded and chopped
- 3/4 C. green onions, green tops and bulbs, chopped
- 2 jalapeno peppers, seeded and finely chopped
- 2 T. fresh lime juice
- 1 C. fresh pineapple, diced
- 2 T. cilantro, snipped
- 1/4 tsp. sea salt

Mix all the ingredients together and chill. For a finely chopped salsa use the food processor for all the ingredients on a quick pulse.
Yield: 3 to 4 cups

Tomato Sauce
Great basic. Who needs a bottle?

- 1/4 C. olive oil
- 1/2 C. red wine
- 2 T. red wine vinegar
- 1/4 C. garlic, minced
- 4 1/2 lb. tomatoes, chopped, plum if possible, seeded and peeled, save the juices
- 1/4 C. tomato paste
- 4 sprigs fresh basil
- 1 C. fresh basil, chopped
- 1 T. sugar
- 1 tsp. fresh oregano
- 1/4 tsp. sea salt
- 1/8 tsp. pepper

Heat olive oil in a saucepan. Add garlic, and sauté for just a few seconds. Add tomatoes, basil sprigs, and all the remaining ingredients except fresh basil. Simmer for 25 minutes, partially covered. Add chopped basil at the end and cook about 5 minutes more. Add salt and pepper.
Yield: 2 quarts

Turkey Gravy

- 2 1/4 C. collected pan juices from a roasted turkey
- 2 C. GF chicken or turkey broth, see Two flowers recipe
- 1 T. cornstarch mixed with 2 T. milk or water
- 1/4 tsp. onion powder
- 1/4 tsp. garlic powder
- 1/4 tsp. poultry seasoning, see Two Flowers recipe
- Sea salt and black pepper to taste

Whisk pan juices with broth, cornstarch, poultry seasoning, salt and pepper. Add remaining ingredients. Cook over low heat, whisking until thickened. Yield: about 4 1/2 cups

Vegetable Herb Sauce
Another good chicken or fish sauce

- 4 oz. unsalted butter
- 1 1/2 C. sliced mushrooms
- 16 artichoke hearts, quartered, drained
- 2 tomatoes, seeded and chopped
- 4 C. GF chicken broth, see Two Flowers recipe
- 1 1/2 C. cold water
- 4 T. cornstarch, 6T. if sauce is to be used over pasta
- 1/4 C. lemon juice
- 1 T. fresh basil, chopped

If you are using frozen artichokes, thaw them. Sauté mushrooms, add artichokes, tomatoes and chicken broth. Bring to a boil. Dissolve cornstarch in water and mix. Simmer until slightly thickened. Add lemon juice and basil. Serve over chicken veal, and pasta. Yield: 4 1/2 cups

Vegetable Pasta Sauce
For the "meatless Monday" pasta meal

4 C. tomatoes, diced, seeded
4 T. olive oil
1 C. red wine
1 C. each: All sliced
Bell pepper
Yellow squash
Red pepper
Zucchini
Sweet onion
Eggplant, peeled and cubed
1 1/2 C. sliced mushrooms
1 C. black olives, sliced
3 garlic cloves, minced
2 T. GF Italian seasoning, see
   Two Flowers recipe
1 tsp. red pepper flakes
1/4 C. fresh basil, chopped
1/4 C. Italian parsley, chopped

Sauté all vegetable slices except mushrooms and tomatoes in olive oil until softened but not "gushy". Add all the seasonings to the vegetables except parsley and fresh basil. Set aside the vegetables. In a deep pan heat the tomatoes, mushrooms and wine until they are soft but still hold together. Add the olives, basil and parsley. Combine the vegetables with the second batch of ingredients and heat through. Serve over rice pasta. Yield: about 8 cups

Watermelon Salsa
Great with chicken or as a dip

2 C. seedless watermelon, cubed
1/4 C. yellow peppers, diced
2 green onion tops and bulbs,
   sliced
1 T. cilantro, chopped
1 tsp. fresh ginger, peeled and
   grated
2 tsp. sweet red wine, optional
1 tsp. fresh lime juice
1/4 tsp. sea salt
1 jalapeno pepper, seeded,
   sliced and minced

Combine watermelon, peppers and onions. Add the seasonings. Mix well and chill. Yield: about 2 1/2 cups

White Clam Sauce

- 4 T. onions, minced
- 2 tsp. garlic, minced
- 2 tsp. olive oil
- 1 C. pure clam juice, bottled
- 3 T. whole milk or cream
- 1 T. cornstarch
- 1/8 tsp. white pepper
- 2 C. clams, chopped

Garnish:
- 2 T. parsley, chopped
- 2 T. Parmesan cheese, grated

Sauté onion and garlic in olive oil until golden brown. Combine juices and milk in a saucepan and simmer. Mix cornstarch with 1 tablespoon water to dissolve. Add to juice mixture. Cook over low heat until thickened. Add this mixture to onions and season to taste. Stir in clams and heat through. Serve over a GF pasta. Yield: 3 cups

Soups & Salads

Baked Potato Soup

3 large baking potatoes, cleaned
1/4 C. unsalted butter
1/2 C. sweet onion, chopped
2 garlic cloves, minced
1/4 C. GF all purpose flour, see Two Flowers recipe
1/4 C. unsalted butter
2 C. chicken broth, see Two Flowers recipe
1 C. whole milk
1/2 C. whipping cream
2 tsp. sea salt
4 slices GF bacon, fried and drained
8 oz. cheddar cheese, shredded
Sour cream for topping

Bake potatoes in oven or microwave. Cool. Dice potatoes. Sauté onions and garlic in butter until tender. Set aside. Melt butter and add flour. Stir well to make a roux. Add milk a little at a time to make a thick sauce. Mix sauce with the potatoes, bacon and seasonings. Add chicken broth and continue to heat until it thickens. Stir in shredded cheese and stir until it melts in the soup. Add sour cream for garnish after soup is in the bowl. Yield: 4 servings

Beefy Broth

4 lbs. short ribs or beef bones
2 lbs. of soup bones ordered from meat department
1 gal. of water
2 C. red wine
5 garlic cloves, peeled and left whole
2 C. carrots, chopped
2 C. onions, peeled and chopped
2 C. celery, chopped
1/2 C. parsley, chopped
1 tsp. salt
1/2 tsp. black pepper
5 bay leaves

In a roasting pan, put bones and ribs in a 450° oven. Roast meat and bones for 30 minutes, uncovered. Skim fat off the roasted beef. Spread vegetables over the top of the bones and roast for 30 minutes more, uncovered. Empty the bones and vegetables into a stock pot. Add water, wine and seasonings. Cook on the stove for 4 to 5 hours lightly covered. Skim off foam as it cooks. Once it is fully cooked strain out the solids and refrigerate overnight. Skim off fat. Broth is ready for use. You can use the beef from the ribs to add to soups and for beef flavoring. Store in a glass jars with lids or freeze in smaller amounts for later use. Yield: about 4 quarts

Brie and Asparagus Soup

- 1 lb. fresh asparagus, cut into slices
- 1 C. unsalted butter
- 1/2 C. GF all purpose flour, see Two Flowers recipe
- 6 C. chicken broth, see Two Flowers recipe
- 2 C. heavy cream
- 1 C. white wine
- 12 oz. Brie, rind removed
- 1/4 tsp. sea salt
- 1/4 tsp. white pepper

Sauté asparagus in butter until soft. Save 1/4 cup asparagus for garnish. Stir in flour until mix turns light brown. Cook and stir for 2 minutes. Gradually add broth, cream and wine. Bring to a boil and simmer for 10 minutes. Cool slightly and process mixture until smooth. Return processed mixture to saucepan and add cubed Brie. Whisk mixture until Brie is melted. Add saved asparagus to garnish. Yield: 8 cups

Black Bean Soup

- 2 strips thick cut GF bacon, diced, save the drippings
- 1 C. sweet onion, diced
- 2 T. garlic, minced
- 2 tsp. paprika
- 1 tsp. cumin
- 1 tsp. oregano
- 1/2 tsp. coriander
- 1/4 tsp. cayenne pepper
- 1 T. red wine vinegar
- 2 C. GF chicken broth, see Two Flowers recipe
- 1 1/2 C. tomatoes, diced, save the juice
- 1 lb. black beans, cooked
- 2 T. canola oil
- 1/4 tsp. sea salt
- 1/8 tsp. pepper
- 1/2 C. manchego or jack cheese, shredded
- 1/2 C. sour cream
- jalapeno jelly, optional

See Two Flowers recipe for cooking beans. In a saucepan cook the diced bacon. Drain the bacon on a paper towel and save the drippings in the pan. Swirl the vinegar in the pan to deglaze it. Sauté the onions and seasonings in the drippings. When onions are soft stir in the tomatoes and 1 cup of broth. Bring mixture to a boil. Puree 1/2 the cooked beans until smooth. Stir in the pureed beans and the whole beans. Simmer to heat the soup through. Garnish with the cheese, sour cream and a dollop of jelly. Yield 8 cups.

Cheesy Onion Soup

1 C. sweet onion. chopped
3 T. unsalted butter
3 T. GF all purpose flour, see Two Flowers recipe
1/2 tsp. sea salt
1/8 tsp. pepper
4 C. whole milk
16 oz. sharp cheddar cheese, shredded
Parmesan, shaved for top

Sauté onion in butter. Stir in flour and seasonings. Blend well. Add milk gradually. Bring to a boil. Cook and stir until thick. Stir in cheese until fully melted. Sprinkle shaved Parmesan cheese on top. Yield: 6 Cups

Chicken Noodle Soup
Nothing but pure comfort

6 C. chicken broth, see Two Flowers recipe
2 C. chicken, cooked and shredded
2 T. olive oil
2 ribs celery, chopped
2 carrots. chopped
1 leek, finely sliced
2 bay leaves
2 T. parsley, chopped
3 C. GF noodles, cooked, see Two Flowers recipe

In olive oil sauté celery, leeks, carrots until softened. Bring the broth to a simmer and add the cooked chicken, sautéed vegetables, and seasonings. Simmer for 25 to 30 minutes. Add the cooked noodles and parsley. Heat through. Serve. Yield: 6 to 8 cups
You can adapt this recipe by adding rice or quinoa.

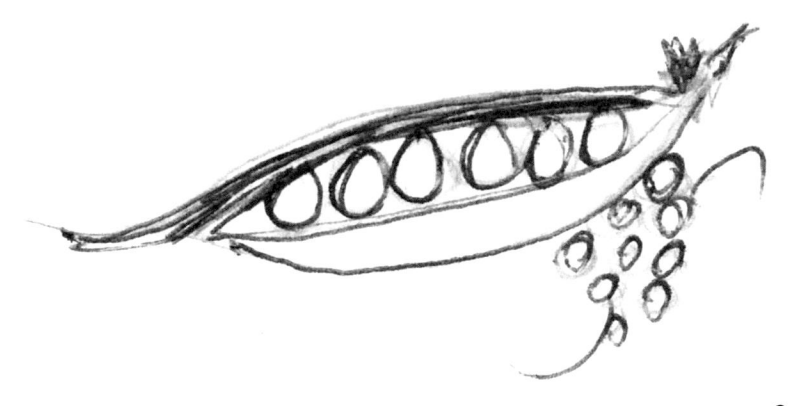

Chicken Stock

- 3 lbs. ground chicken, easier to use than chicken parts and bones
- 1 T. olive oil
- 6 chicken wings, uncooked
- 4 stalks celery, cut in half, greens included
- 2 large white onions, peeled and quartered
- 4 bay leaves
- 10 whole peppercorns
- 1 tsp. sea salt
- 1 gallon water
- 2 C. white wine - optional. Replace with water if not using wine.
- 2 carrots - optional. If you want a clear, not tinged with orange broth do not use carrots.

Brown the ground chicken in a large skillet. Remove the chicken. Pour the drippings into the main stock pot. Stir a few tablespoons of water into the skillet. Bring the water to a boil. Add the vegetables, browned chicken and uncooked wings. Add the wine and seasonings. Simmer on the stove for two hours with cover vented. Can remove any white foam wtih a slotted spoon while it is simmering. Strain out the cooked vegetables and chicken and refrigerate overnight. Skim off fat. Stock is now ready to use. Store stock in glass jars or freeze in cup sized servings for future use.

Corn and Chicken Chowder

- 6 slices cooked bacon, set aside, reserve 2T. of drippings
- 1 lb. chicken breast cubes, uncooked
- 1/2 C. sweet onion, chopped
- 1/2 C. sweet peppers, chopped
- 1 garlic clove, minced
- 4 C. GF chicken broth, see Two Flowers recipe
- 2 C. corn, whole kernel, fresh or frozen
- 2 C. corn, creamed, frozen
- 1/4 C. cornstarch
- 1/2 tsp. sea salt
- 1/4 tsp. pepper
- 1 1/2 C. jack cheese or hot pepper cheese, shredded

Heat bacon drippings. Add chicken, onion, sweet peppers, and garlic. Fully cook chicken, no pink showing, with onion and peppers until soft. Add chicken broth, and both corn ingredients. Combine cornstarch and milk in a bowl. Stir it into the soup. Bring the soup to boil and simmer 15 minutes to blend flavors. Add seasonings and cheese. Mix until cheese is melted. Top with bacon. Yield: 6 Cups

Corn and Quinoa Soup

3 red peppers, cubed
1/4 C. sweet onion, diced
1 C. red quinoa
1 T. unsalted butter
1 T. olive oil
2 garlic cloves, minced
1/3 C. GF all purpose flour, see Two Flowers recipe

4 C. GF chicken broth, see Two Flowers Recipe
2 C. heavy cream
20 oz. frozen corn, thawed
1 1/2 C. black beans, cooked
2 T. parsley, chopped
1 tsp. salt
1/2 tsp. pepper

See Two Flowers recipe for cooking dried beans. Broil the peppers until they blister. Cube them. In a skillet melt the butter and olive oil. Add garlic and cook garlic until soft. Blend in flour. Whisk in broth and cream. Add corn, beans, peppers, and quinoa. Heat but do not boil. Simmer for about 20 minutes, stirring frequently. Make sure the quinoa and vegetables are fully cooked. Stir in all remaining ingredients. Yield: 6 cups

Creamy, NO Cream, Cauliflower Soup

2 T. unsalted butter
1 C. onions, diced
2 T. white wine
5 C. fresh cauliflower florets
1 tsp. coriander
2 C. chicken broth, see Two Flowers recipe

1 tsp. salt
1/4 tsp. white pepper
2 tsp. tarragon, minced
1/2 C. almond milk for thinning
1/8 C. chives, chopped

Sauté onion in butter until soft. Add wine. Add broth, salt and pepper. Chop cauliflower and add to broth. Cook cauliflower until tender about 15 minutes to 20 minutes. Cool soup. Puree soup in the food processor. Thin with almond milk. Garnish with chives. Yield: 6 servings

Creamy Spinach, Mushroom and Wild Rice Soup

4 Slices GF Bacon
1/3 C. green onions, bulbs and tops, sliced
1/3 C. carrot, diced
1 10 oz. pkg. frozen spinach, thawed
2 garlic cloves, minced
3 C. GF chicken broth, see Two Flowers recipe
1/2 C. wild rice, do not use seasoning if this is a boxed item
2 C. mushrooms of choice, sliced
1/4 C. unsalted butter
1/4 C. GF all purpose flour, see Two Flowers recipe
3 C. milk or heavy cream

Sauté all the ingredients, except wild rice, with the raw bacon. When vegetables are tender chop everything into small pieces. In a saucepan melt butter, add flour. Mix well with a wooden spoon. Add chicken broth, a little at a time, so there are no lumps. Incorporate the two mixes and cook over medium heat. Add more chicken broth if the mixture becomes too thick. Add cooked rice. Yield: 6 to 8 Cups

Egg Drop Soup

4 C. GF chicken broth, see Two Flowers recipe
1 T. ginger, sliced
4 green onions, bulbs and tops, sliced
2 T. sherry, not cooking sherry
1 tsp. sesame oil
1 C. chicken breast, cubes, uncooked
4 T. cornstarch
1 tsp. sea salt
1/8 tsp. pepper
3 large eggs, beaten

Simmer chicken broth with ginger and onions until ginger is soft. Strain out the onions and ginger. Toss 1 tablespoon cornstarch, salt and pepper with chicken breast cubes. Thicken broth with 3 tablespoons of cornstarch. Add chicken breast cubes and cook for 3 minutes until fully cooked. Slowly add beaten eggs in a steady stream into the chicken broth. The eggs will cook up in threads. Yield: 6 Cups

Farina Ball Soup
Nana's recipe but made gluten free

1 1/4 C. brown rice farina, like Bob's Red Mill Hot and Hardy brown rice farina cereal
4 eggs, beaten
1/4 tsp. sea salt
4 T. melted unsalted butter or 4 T. canola oil

1 T. potato starch
1/4 tsp. xanthan gum
8 cups GF chicken broth, see Two Flowers recipe

Combine farina, salt, potato starch and gum. Mix well. Beat eggs with oil and mix into farina mixture. Put into refrigerator and let it set for 30 minutes. Bring 4 cups of broth to a boil. Lower heat to simmer and drop an egg shaped tablespoon-sized dumpling off your spoon into the simmering chicken broth. Cover and cook for 20 minutes or until centers are soft. Check and make sure the broth is simmering and not boiling. It is important that the broth is barely bubbling as a rapid simmer will break the dumplings apart. Use the rest of the broth to ladle into bowls. Yield: at least 6 servings

Fresh Mushroom Soup

6 C. fresh mushrooms
1/2 C. unsalted butter
2 C. sweet onions, chopped
1 T. brown sugar
1/4 C. GF all purpose flour, see Two Flowers recipe

1 C. water
2 C. GF chicken broth, see Two Flowers recipe
1/2 tsp. sea salt
1/4 tsp. pepper
1/2 C. parsley, chopped

Quarter 1/2 the mushrooms and chop the rest. Brown onion and brown sugar in butter. Cook until onions are caramelized. Add mushrooms and sauté 5 minutes. Add flour and stir until smooth. Add seasonings. Cook 1 minute. Gradually add water and broth. Cook over medium heat until thickened. Garnish with parsley. Yield: 6 to 8 cups

Fresh Tomato Broth

- 4 C. tomatoes, chopped, with juice and seeds
- 2 T. olive oil
- 1/2 C. carrot, chopped
- 1/2 C. celery, chopped
- 1/2 C. onion, chopped
- 2 garlic cloves, chopped
- 1/2 C. dry white wine, you can substitute 1/4 C. white wine vinegar
- 1 T. fresh basil leaves, chopped
- 2 C. GF chicken or GF vegetable broth, see Two Flowers recipe
- 1 tsp. sea salt
- 1/2 tsp. black pepper

Heat oil in a heavy-bottomed pot over medium heat. Add chopped vegetables and cook until softened about 10 minutes. Add garlic and cook a few minutes more. Add wine or vinegar to scrape up the bottom of the pan. Stir in the tomatoes and basil. Simmer until the broth thickens. Strain out the vegetables and add salt and pepper. Yield 6 cups

Peachy Cold Soup

- 4 C. peach nectar
- 4 T. apple juice concentrate, thawed
- 5 T. cornstarch
- 2 1/2 C. dry white wine
- 4 T. honey
- 10 cups fresh peaches, pureed
- 1/2 C. peach liqueur
- 1/2 C. almonds
- 1/2 C. Greek yogurt
- 1/2 C. sour cream

Bring nectar, 2 cups of wine, juices, and honey to a boil. Simmer. Dissolve cornstarch in remaining 1/2 cup wine. Whisk the mixture into simmering liquid. Cook, whisking gently until the liquid is clear and smooth. Remove from heat and add more honey if necessary. Cool to room temperature. Process peaches and add almonds to puree. Stir the peach mixture into the thickened wine mixture. Drizzle in liqueur. Whisk in yogurt and sour cream and chill. Yield: 9 cups

Red Lentil Soup

2 tsp. olive oil
1 C. carrots, chopped
1/2 C. sweet onion, chopped
2 tsp. fresh ginger, grated
1 tsp. garlic clove, minced
1 1/2 tsp. curry powder, optional
1/4 tsp. coarse sea salt
1/4 tsp. pepper

4 C. GF chicken broth, see Two Flowers recipe
1 lb. red lentils, rinsed
2 C. tomatoes, diced
Garnish:
1 C. Parmesan cheese, slivered
1/4 C. parsley, chopped

No need to soak lentils. Sauté onions and carrots in a saucepan. Cook until soft. Add ginger and garlic with the seasonings. Cook for a few minutes. Stir in broth and bring the mixture to a boil. Add red lentils and simmer, covered, for 30 minutes. I like the red lentils because the red color makes a more appetizing soup. Make sure the lentils are tender. Stir in the tomatoes and cook until they are heated through. Put soup into bowls and garnish with the parsley and cheese. Yield: 4 to 6 servings

Roasted Red Pepper and Eggplant Bisque
Kara Koprowski

3 T. unsalted butter
1 C. sweet yellow onion, diced
2 T. garlic, minced
6 C. roasted red peppers, peeled and coarsely chopped
2 medium sized eggplants, peeled and chopped into same size as peppers
6 C. chicken or vegetable stock, see Two Flowers recipe
4 dashes hot pepper sauce such as Tabasco
2 C. half and half cream
Salt and pepper to taste, about 1 tsp. of each

See note below regarding roasting bell peppers. If you are using roasted peppers in a jar, discard the liquid. In a large stock pot, melt butter. Add onion and garlic and sauté 5 minutes or until softened. Add red peppers and eggplant. Sauté an additional 10 minutes until all vegetables golden brown. Add stock and cook uncovered over medium heat until soup begins to simmer. Reduce heat to low. Cook on low uncovered for 20 minutes until vegetables are tender and fragrant. Add seasonings to taste. Using an immersion blender puree until smooth in the stock pot. Also can transfer to blender and puree in batches. Do not fill blender more than 3/4 full since bisque will expand because it is warm. If using blender, pour bisque back into stockpot. Add half and half and simmer over low heat until warm. Do not boil. Will keep in refrigerator for 2 to 3 days. Can also be frozen. Yield: 4 to 6 servings

Note about roasted bell peppers: 5 fresh bell peppers should yield 6 cups of roasted peppers. Peppers can be roasted in a 450° oven, over an open gas flame, under the broiler or on top of stove using a grill pan until skins are black and blistered. Place in a bowl covered with plastic wrap or in a plastic bag for 15 minutes. Peel skin from peppers; remove seeds and stem.

Shrimp and Spinach Soup

4 C. GF chicken broth, see Two Flowers recipe
3 C. red skinned potato chunks
1/2 C. sweet onions, shredded
1/2 C. carrots, peeled and shredded
1 tsp. sea salt
1/2 tsp. pepper
1/4 tsp. nutmeg
6 T. unsalted butter
6 T. white rice flour
1 C. milk
8 C. spinach leaves, slivered, stems removed
1/2 lb. shrimp, cleaned and deveined, cut in half
2 C. heavy cream
1 T. lemon zest
Few drops of GF hot sauce

Simmer potatoes, onions, carrots in broth with seasonings for 20 minutes. While the potato mixture is simmering, melt the butter in a saucepan and whisk in the rice flour until it is smooth. Whisk in the milk. Stir the contents of the saucepan into the simmering potato mixture. Cook for several minutes. Add shrimp and cook until shrimp turns a light pink color. Toss in the spinach and cook just until it softens. Remove from heat and stir in cream, zest and hot sauce. Yield: 6 to 8 servings

Shrimp Bisque Velvet
Yes, you will be using the shells

- 2 lbs. shell-on Gulf shrimp, no foreign or pond raised
- 3 T. olive oil
- 1/2 C. brandy, warmed
- 2 T. unsalted butter
- 4 T. carrot, grated
- 4 T. celery, grated
- 6 T. onion, grated
- 1/2 C. GF all purpose flour, see Two Flowers recipe
- 1 1/2 C. white wine
- 4 C. bottled pure clam juice
- 2 C. Roma or plum tomatoes, chopped
- 1/4 tsp. fresh tarragon, minced
- 1 C. whipping cream
- 1 T. lemon juice
- 2 T. sherry, not cooking sherry
- 1/2 tsp. sea salt
- 1/4 tsp. white pepper

Peel half the shrimp and save the shells. Cut the peeled shrimp into small pieces. Reserve. Dry all the shrimp and shells with paper towels. In a large skillet, heat half the oil. Add half of the shell-on shrimp and half of the shells to the hot oil. Cook until shrimp and shells turn a pink color. Repeat with the rest of the shrimp and shells. Add brandy and ignite the brandy so alcohol burns off. Cool mixture. Transfer shrimp mixture to the food processor and process until the shrimp and shells become sandy in texture. Set aside. In another large saucepan, heat butter. Add carrot, onion, celery and ground shrimp mixture. Cook until all the vegetables are soft. Add flour and combine. Stir in clam juice, wine and tomatoes stirring the mixture. Cover and bring to a boil. Turn down the heat and simmer until soup thickens. Strain the soup, pressing all the juices from the solids. Discard solids. Clean out the pan. Return the strained soup to the pan and add cream, lemon juice. Add reserved cut shrimp and simmer until shrimp are firm. Stir in the sherry. Yield: 6 cups

Split Pea Soup Updated
This swings well into vegetarian

1 1/2 C. onions, chopped
1 C. celery, chopped with tops
2 C. carrots, chopped
1 C. red skins potatoes, diced, not peeled
1 lb. dry split peas, rinsed
2 garlic cloves, minced
1/4 C. olive oil

1 bay leaf
Dash of allspice
1/4 tsp. marjoram
1/4 C. parsley, chopped
8 C. GF chicken broth, see Two Flowers recipe
1 1/2 pounds of GF ham, cottage ham, hocks, or bits from a bone

No need to soak peas. Rinse, drain and look through peas for small stones. Rinse the peas. Sauté onion, garlic, celery, and carrots in olive oil with spices. Cook until soft. Add peas, potatoes, ham choice and chicken broth. Simmer with bay leaf, uncovered until peas start to thicken. Skim off foam as you go along. Stir in parsley at the end. Salt and pepper to your taste. The ham may offer enough salt, so taste before you salt. Yield: 8 cups

Summertime Vegetable Soup

- 1 lb. fresh asparagus, trimmed
- 6 T. unsalted butter
- 2 green onions, tops and bulbs, chopped
- 6 C. chicken broth, see Two Flowers recipe
- 1 lb. fresh spinach, whole, stems removed
- 2 1/2 T. GF all purpose flour, see Two Flowers recipe
- 1/4 tsp. sea salt
- 1/8 tsp. white pepper
- 1 C. peas, fresh or frozen
- 1 C. snap peas, fresh or frozen, cut in half
- 1/2 C. milk
- 1 C. Boston or bibb lettuce, shredded
- 1/8 C. fresh chives, minced
- 1/8 C. fresh watercress, chopped

Cut off tips of asparagus and save. Chop the stalks into small pieces. Melt 2 tablespoons of butter in saucepan and sauté green onions with 1/2 cup broth. Cook for 5 minutes until tender. Add asparagus and cook until tender. Add remaining broth and bring to a boil. Simmer 10 minutes. Add 2 cups spinach. Cook until spinach wilts. Place this mixture in food processor and process until smooth. Heat remaining butter and whisk in flour. Cook 1 minute. Whisk mixture in pureed soup. Add peas, asparagus tips,and snap peas to soup. Simmer a few minutes more so they are still crisp. Stir in milk. DO NOT Boil. Stir in remaining spinach and chopped lettuce that has been shredded. It should still be crisp. Garnish with watercress and chives. Yield: 10 cups

Tex Mex Stew

- 2 C. tomatoes, diced
- 2 tsp. chipolte chile, minced
- 4 sliced GF bacon, cooked and chopped
- 4 lbs. boneless chuck roast, cubed
- 1/4 C. potato starch
- 1 tsp. salt
- 1/2 tsp. pepper
- 1 C. sweet onion, minced
- 1 jalapeno chile, seeded, minced
- 3 T. pure chili powder
- 1 1/2 tsp. ground cumin
- 4 garlic cloves, minced
- 4 C. water
- 2 T. brown sugar
- 2 T. GF corn muffin mix, see Two Flowers recipe

In a food processor puree the tomatoes and chipolte chile until smooth. Set aside. Cook the bacon in a large pan on the stove. Reserve 3 tablespoons of bacon fat for the browning of the meat. Toss the meat in the potato starch. Divide the meat into 2 batches and brown each batch separately in 1 tablespoon of bacon fat. In the third tablespoon of fat brown the onion and the jalapeno chile and cook until softened. Stir in all the other seasonings. Stir in the tomato sauce and water. Add the meat, bacon, and sugar. Bring to a boil, cover and simmer for 1 hour. Skim the fat and cook until the meat is tender at least another hour. Take 1 cup of the liquid and mix in the corn muffin mix to thicken it. Whisk it into the stew and stir until thickened. Yield: 8 cups

Tomato Cream Soup

- 4 C. fresh tomatoes, seeds removed, drained, reserve juice
- 2 T. brown sugar
- 4 T. unsalted butter
- 4 minced shallots
- Few sprinkles of allspice
- Few sprinkles of nutmeg
- 2 T. GF all purpose flour, see Two Flowers recipe
- 2 C. GF chicken broth, see Two Flowers recipe
- 1/2 C. whipping cream
- 2 T. sherry, not cooking sherry
- 1/4 tsp. sea salt
- 1/8 tsp. cayenne pepper

Preheat oven to 400°. Reserve tomato juice to make 3 cups total. Place quartered tomatoes in a single layer on a parchment or foil lined cookie sheet in a 400° oven. Sprinkle brown sugar over them and bake about 30 minutes. These tomatoes will become oven dried. Peel them from the paper and cool. Sauté shallots in melted butter until soft. Add flour and stir until thickened. Whisk in chicken broth, 3 cups tomato juice and roasted tomatoes. Bring to a boil. Once a boil is reached reduce to simmer. Stir and blend flavors for about 10 minutes. Strain out solids and put into a food processor with 1 cup of the liquid and puree mixture. Pour the puree and the remaining liquid into a saucepan. Add cream. Heat but do not boil. Stir in sherry, salt and cayenne. Yield: 6 servings

Very Vegetable Turkey Chili
Kara Koprowski

- 1 lb. ground fresh turkey
- 2 bell peppers, any color, seeded and chopped
- 1 medium sweet yellow onion, chopped
- 2 carrots, peeled and chopped
- 2 garlic cloves, minced
- 1 fresh jalapeno pepper, chopped, seeds removed if desired for less heat
- 8 Roma tomatoes, diced
- 4 C. roasted tomato sauce, see Two Flowers recipe
- 1 C. sweet corn, fresh or frozen, no need to thaw
- 2 C. squash, fresh or frozen, peeled and chopped
- 2 tsp. Worcestershire sauce
- 1 tsp. chili powder
- 1 tsp. ground cumin
- 1 tsp. black pepper
- 1 tsp. salt
- 2 T. bittersweet chocolate chips or any dark chocolate, chopped

Garnishes: optional
Sour cream
Avocado
Shredded cheese

Brown turkey using 2 T. vegetable oil or cooking spray in large pan. Cook and crumble turkey until it is cooked through about 5 to 6 minutes. Drain any fat or liquid and transfer turkey to a crock pot or large stock pot. In same pan, add a few additional tablespoons of vegetable oil. Over medium heat, add bell pepper, onion, carrot, garlic and jalapeno pepper. Sauté until it is light golden brown and fragrant, about 5 minutes. Add cooked turkey to vegetable mixture along with remaining ingredients and seasonings except for chocolate. If mixture is very thick it can be thinned with a small amount of water, vegetable or chicken stock. Cover and cook over medium heat on the stove for about 45 minutes. Stir occasionally. Or, cover and cook on low heat in crock pot for 6 hours. At end of the cooking time add chocolate and stir until chocolate is melted. Can cook an additional 15 minutes on the stove or 30 minutes in the crock pot on low. Add additional salt and pepper to taste. Can serve with sour cream, avocado or cheese if desired. Makes 12 servings.

Vegetable Broth
Easy replacement for store purchased broth

- 2 T. olive oil
- 4 large yellow onions, sliced
- 6 celery stalks, with tops, diced
- 6 medium leeks with tops, cleaned and chopped
- 1 large garlic bulb, separated into cloves, peeled
- 3 large carrots, chopped
- 1 C. chopped flat leaf parsley
- 1 bay leaf
- 1 tsp. sea salt
- 1/2 tsp. black peppercorns
- 4 sprigs fresh thyme
- 2 bay leaves
- 2 plum tomatoes, chopped

Brown vegetables in a heavy-bottomed stockpot, except for tomatoes and leeks in olive oil. Cover and cook over low heat, stirring frequently, until vegetables are caramelized, 20 to 30 minutes. Add leeks and cook covered until leeks soften, about 10 more minutes. Add 10 cups hot water, tomatoes and spices to the vegetables. Cook 30 minutes uncovered. Strain the solids out but do not press or squeeze the solids as the solids will turn your broth a murky color. Stock can be covered and refrigerated up to 4 days. You can freeze stock in smaller portions for later use. Using plastic freezer bags stored flat in the freezer is a great space saver. Try freezing some in ice cube trays.

White Bean Soup with Bacon

- 1 1/2 C. white beans, cooked
- 3 T. olive oil
- 1 C. celery, diced
- 2 C. sweet onions, diced
- 4 C. GF chicken broth, see Two Flowers recipe
- 8 strips GF bacon
- 1/2 tsp. sea salt
- 1/4 tsp. pepper
- 2 T. parsley, minced
- 1/8 tsp. paprika

See the Two Flowers recipe for cooking beans. When cooked pour beans through a strainer and save broth. Cook the bacon. Set aside. Sauté onions and celery. Puree beans and pour beans into a saucepan. Add bacon and sautéed vegetables. Stir. Add bean liquid if soup is too thick. Fresh beans make a nice thick soup. I like to double the recipe so I can freeze servings. Yield: 6 cups

ABC Salad - Apple, Broccoli Cranberry
Kara Koprowski

1/2 C. canola oil
3 T. lemon juice, divided
1 tsp. sugar
1/4 tsp. salt
1 C. dried cranberries or cherries
2 large apples, cut into cubes, Honeycrisp, Fuji or Gala work well
1 head fresh broccoli
1/2 C. walnuts, chopped, can substitute pecans

Place head of broccoli in boiling water for 3 seconds. Transfer to a large bowl of ice water to stop the cooking. This step will eliminate the raw broccoli taste. This step can be omitted. Cut broccoli in small florets.

In a bowl, whisk oil, 2 tablespoons lemon juice, sugar and salt. Add cranberries and let stand for 10 minutes. In another larger bowl, toss apples with remaining lemon juice. Add broccoli, walnuts and cranberry mixture and toss gently. Cover and refrigerate for 2 hours or until chilled. To serve, let stand 15 minutes at room temperature and stir salad before serving. Yield: 6 to 8 servings.

Asian Salad Wraps

Sauce:
1/4 C. GF hoisin sauce, see Two Flowers recipe
1/4 C. fresh lime juice
3 T. GF soy sauce
1 T. light brown sugar
2 T. Asian chili oil, naturally GF
1 T. GF fish sauce
3 tsp. sesame seeds, toasted
Filling:
4 oz. rice stick noodles, cooked according to package directions, drained
1/2 each of a whole red and yellow pepper, cut into matchstick pieces
2 carrots, peeled and cut into matchstick pieces
4 oz. enoki mushrooms, they fit into the wrap the best
2 C. bean sprouts and shoots
16 6" round rice wrappers
16 red or green leaf lettuce leaves, with the core cut out
16 fresh chive strands

Whisk sauce ingredients. Mix sauce into drained noodles and set aside to marinate. Prepare a bowl with warm water. Dip each rice round, one by one, into water to soften. Place softened rounds on a piece of parchment paper. Cover each one with a wet paper towel while you work on softening the remaining wraps. Use one lettuce leaf on each round and add the noodle mixture, then the vegetables on top of the lettuce. Do not go to the edge. Leave a larger edge on the bottom. Starting at the bottom, flap the bottom up over the filled wrap. Gently, but tightly roll up the sides of the wrap and secure it with a long chive strand. Place the finished wrap on a platter and cover with a wet towel. Refrigerate up to 2 hours before serving. Yield: 8 servings of 2 wraps each

Avocado Lemon Shrimp Salad

- 2 lb. peeled, cleaned shrimp with tails removed
- 3 lemons cut into wedges
- 2 tsp. black pepper

Dressing:
- 4 red grapefruit, peeled and cut into wedges, juice saved
- 2 avocados, peeled and sliced
- 4 T. fresh lime juice
- 1 tsp. honey
- 3 tsp. fresh ginger, peeled and grated
- 1 tsp. sea salt
- 1/4 tsp. black pepper
- 2 T. fresh mint, chopped

Salad:
- 1 C. snap peas with ends cut off, slivered
- Lettuce of choice such as romaine or butter lettuce, washed and torn in bite sized pieces, about 6 large handfuls.

Bring 6 cups of water to a boil. Squeeze lemon wedges and add to water. Boil water and lemons for a few minutes. Turn off heat and add shrimp. Let shrimp poach for 5 minutes if fresh or 10 minutes if frozen. Drain, discarding lemons. Add cooked shrimp to a bowl filled with ice. As soon as shrimp are cooled, drain and refrigerate.

Vinaigrette:
In a blender place reserved grapefruit juice and enough water to make 1/2 cup of liquid. Puree the remaining ingredients and 1 avocado to make the dressing. Toss together the remaining avocado, grapefruit slices, and shrimp. Pour dressing over the shrimp, avocado and grapefruit mixture and gently toss. Serve shrimp mixture over lettuce and snap peas. Yield: 6 dinner sized servings.

Avocado Salad

Salad:
- 3 ripe avocados, peeled and diced
- 3 firm tomatoes, diced
- 3/4 C. Nicoise olives, chopped
- 3 hard cooked eggs, sliced
- 1 /4 C. red onion, sliced
- 1 1/2 C. favorite GF corn chips, crushed

Dressing:
- 2 T. parsley, minced
- 1/2 C. white wine vinegar
- 1/2 C. olive oil
- 2 tsp. cumin
- salt and pepper to taste
- 1 tsp. paprika

Prepare dressing in a blender. Add salt and pepper to taste. Gently toss dressing with avocados, tomatoes, and olives. Put salad into a bowl to serve 6. Top with chopped eggs and red onion. Sprinkle chips around the bowl. Yield: 6 servings

Brown Rice with Tomatoes and Basil Salad

- 1 C. brown rice. not instant
- 2 tsp. sea salt
- 1 garlic clove, minced
- 2 C. tomatoes, seeded and diced, firm tomatoes work best
- 1/4 C. rice wine vinegar
- 1 T. sugar
- 1 T. olive oil
- 1 C. fresh basil leaves, chopped, no stems

Cook rice according to package directions until tender. Cool to room temperature. Stir in tomatoes. Whisk all other ingredients together and pour over the rice. Stir in basil. Yield: 4 to 6 cups

Buckwheat Noodle Salad

16 oz. buckwheat noodles, cooked, run under cold water and drained
Dressing:
1/4 C. rice vinegar
2 T. ginger, grated
1 T. honey
2 T. GF soy sauce
2 tsp. sesame oil
2 T. GF chili sauce
1/4 C. canola oil

Salad Additions:
1/2 C. carrot, grated
1 red pepper, sliced
1 cucumber, sliced and quartered
4 green onions, tops and bulbs, sliced
1/4 C. parsley, chopped

Whisk dressing ingredients well in a small bowl. Mix into noodles. Add the vegetables and mix again. Allow salad to sit 10 minutes so the noodles absorb the dressing. Yield: 6 servings

Cellophane Noodle Salad with Shrimp and Chicken

1 lb. cellophane noodles, uncooked
1/2 C. celery, diced
3/4 C. radishes, sliced
1 1/2 C. English cucumber, slivered
1/4 C. green onions, bulbs and tops, sliced
1/2 C. parsley, minced
1/2 C. peanuts, chopped, not dry roasted
1 lb. chicken breasts, cut into strips

1 lb. shrimp, uncooked
1 T. olive oil
Rice flour to coat shrimp and chicken
Dressing:
1/4 C. GF soy sauce
3 T. lime juice
1/2 tsp. GF hot sauce
1 T. fresh ginger, minced
3 T. sugar
2 T. GF fish sauce

Cook noodles and cool. Add all the vegetables. Reserve peanuts. Whisk dressing and pour over noodles. Let noodles sit to absorb dressing. Meanwhile coat chicken and shrimp with rice flour and fry quickly until cooked. Cool. Add to noodle salad and garnish with peanuts. Yield: 4 to 6 servings

Chinese Chicken Salad

- 1 C. plain Greek yogurt
- 1 T. GF smooth peanut butter
- 1 T. rice wine vinegar
- 1 tsp. sesame oil
- 1 garlic clove, minced
- 3 C. cooked, cubed chicken breast
- 1/2 C. orange segments
- 6 green onions, tops and bulbs, sliced
- 1 red pepper, thinly sliced
- 1 small can water chestnuts, sliced, drained
- 2 C. cellophane noodles, cooked and cooled
- 4 C. mixed greens
- 4 tsp. sunflower seeds, salted

Mix yogurt, peanut butter, vinegar, oil and garlic together. Pour it over the cooked noodles. Add the vegetables to the noodles. Add chicken and oranges. Mix well. Refrigerate for flavors to set. Serve over greens. Yield: 4 to 6 servings

Cold Asian Noodles

- 1 lb. cooked chicken breast, cooled and cut into strips
- 1 C. GF baked ham, cut into strips
- 6 green onions, bulbs and tops, cut into strips
- 1/2 C. toasted walnuts, chopped
- 8 oz. Chinese rice stick noodles, cooked and drained
- 1 1/2 C. canola oil
- 2 1/2 T. sesame oil
- 2 T. sesame seeds
- 3 T. coriander seeds, crushed
- 3/4 C. GF soy sauce
- 1 tsp. hot GF Asian chili oil
- 2 tsp. sugar

Mix the chicken, ham, onions and walnuts in a bowl. Add the rice sticks. Heat the oil and seeds in a small sauce pan over medium heat until the seeds are light brown. Take the pan off the heat and stir in the soy and coriander. Stir in the chili oil and sugar. Keep heating until the sauce thickens a little. Pour sauce over the noodle mixture and then refrigerate the noodle salad and serve cold. Yield: 4 servings

Cold Beet Salad

Dressing:
1/2 C. orange juice
4 T. olive oil
1 T. white champagne vinegar
1/4 tsp. sea salt
1/2 tsp. pepper

Salad:
2 1/2 C. salad greens
3 C. cooked beets, diced, use striped beets
2/3 C. walnuts toasted
1/2 tsp. sugar
2/3 C. blue cheese, crumbled

Preheat oven to 350°. to make dressing, pour orange juice, oil, vinegar and seasonings into a blender. Pulse until it thickens. Set aside. Cook beets and cool them down. While beets are cooling, toast the walnuts in a 350° oven until lightly browned. While the nuts are still warm toss with the sugar. Layer the cooled beets over the greens and sprinkle with blue cheese and walnuts. Pour dressing over the salad and serve. Yield: 4 servings

Cornbread Salad

2 C. GF cornbread, see Two Flowers recipe
1/4 C. Parmesan cheese, grated
1/2 C. cilantro, chopped
1/2 C. red onions, slivered
4 firm tomatoes, chopped, seeded
1/4 C. GF red wine vinegar
1 T. olive oil
1/4 tsp. sea salt
1/4 tsp. pepper

Cube and toast cornbread in a 400° oven. Toss cubes in Parmesan cheese when crisp. Add onion, tomatoes and cilantro to cubes. Whisk all other ingredients together and pour over bread mixture. Let the salad sit for at least 10 minutes so the cornbread absorbs the dressing. Yield: 4 servings

Fresh Tropical Fruit Salad with Lemon Banana Dressing

Kara Koprowski

Dressing:
- 2 medium sized ripe bananas, peeled and sliced
- 1 C. Greek vanilla or lemon yogurt, not lite
- 2 T. honey
- 3 tsp. fresh lemon or orange juice

Salad: 8 C. fruit, cut
- Mango
- Papaya
- Kiwi
- Pineapple
- Starfruit
- Honeydew
- Cantaloupe
- Strawberries
- Blueberries
- Blackberries
- Raspberries
- 1/2 C. almonds or walnuts, toasted, optional

Use at least 6 kinds of tropical and conventional fruit. In a blender, combine dressing ingredients. Blend over low speed until smooth. Chill covered for up to 3 hours. The fruit is best served on individual plates so that it can be arranged but you can serve from a large bowl if desired. Pour dressing over fruit salad mixture. To toast nuts, place them in a dry skillet over medium heat. Toss nuts in pan until fragrant. Sprinkle toasted nuts on top of dressing. Note: If using bananas in your fruit salad, toss with fresh lemon juice to prevent them from turning brown. Keep fruit salad covered until serving. Yield: 8 servings.

Mango Slaw

- 3 C. cabbage, red and green mixed, shredded
- 1 tsp. salt
- 1/4 C. GF mayonnaise, see Two Flowers recipe
- 1/2 tsp. sugar
- 1/2 tsp. salt
- 1 T. lime juice
- 1 Granny Smith apple, peeled and shredded
- 1 carrot, peeled and shredded
- 1 mango, peeled and thin sliced
- 1/4 C. red onion, thin sliced or shredded

Place cabbage in strainer set over a bowl and sprinkle with salt. Let cabbage drain for about 15 minutes to dry it out. Squeeze out the cabbage in a towel to get it as dry as possible. Toss the cabbage with all the other ingredients and let it stand at room temperature for at least 15 minutes before serving. Yield: 4 to 6 servings

Nana's Potato Salad
Gladys Nosse

- 4 lbs. russet potatoes, peeled, not sliced
- 4 T. cider vinegar
- 1 C. chopped celery, include some of the tops
- 4 T. sweet onion, chopped
- 1/4 C. GF sweet pickle relish
- 1 C. GF mayonnaise see Two Flowers recipe
- 1 1/2 tsp. powdered dry mustard
- 1 1/2 tsp. celery seed
- 2 T. salt
- 1 tsp. salt
- 1/4 C. parsley leaves, minced
- 1/2 tsp. black pepper
- 6 eggs, hard boiled and diced

Quarter peeled uncooked potatoes. Immediately put them into a saucepan and completely cover them with water. Bring them to a boil. Add 2 tablespoons salt to the water. Cook the potatoes until tender about 10 minutes. Drain potatoes and transfer them to a bowl. Add vinegar and gently coat the potatoes. Let cool. In another bowl stir all the remaining ingredients except the eggs and including the remaining 1 teasoon of salt to make a dressing. Using a silicone spatula gently fold the dressing into the potatoes. Lastly fold in the diced eggs. Refrigerate covered. Nana also made this potato salad by boiling the potatoes with the skins on. When they were soft, the skins would fall off. Yield: about 12 cups

Quinoa Salad with Cherries and Cashews
Doubles as a vegetarinan entree as well as a side salad

1/2 C. water
1/2 C. orange juice
2/3 C. quinoa, uncooked, red quinoa is nice for the color
1/4 tsp. salt
1/2 C. cashews
1/2 C. dried apricots, slivered
1 C. fresh cherries or assorted grapes, can also use dried fruit of your choice
1/4 C. red onion, chopped
4 C. lettuce leaves, torn

Dressing:
2 T. fresh ginger, grated
1/4 C. honey
2 T. white wine vinegar
2 T lime juice
1 small garlic clove, minced
1/4 C. olive oil

Rinse quinoa and cook in the orange juice and water mixture. Cool 10 minutes. Make honey vinaigrette and mix with all other ingredients, except lettuce. let dressing sit on the salad a few minutes so the ingredients absorb the dressing. Spread quinoa mixture over the torn lettuce leaves. Yield: 4 cups

Rice and Asparagus Orange Salad

2 1/2 C. wild rice, rinsed
4 lb. thin asparagus spears
1/4 tsp. sea salt
Dressing:
2/3 C. orange juice
1/4 red wine vinegar
3 T. orange zest, grated
1/3 C. fresh tarragon
4 seedless oranges, peeled and cut into wheels
1 C. green onions, sliced
2 C. pecans, toasted
10 romaine lettuce leaves, separated
1/2 C. dried cherries

Cook the rice according to the package directions. Do not use the seasoning if this is a boxed item. Clean the asparagus ends. Cut asparagus into 2 inch sections. Steam them until crispy but tender. Drain under cold water or drop into ice water in order to stop the cooking process. Sprinkle them with sea salt. Let them sit on paper towels for a few minutes. Prepare the dressing in a blender. To the cooled rice add the dressing and mix well. Add the pecans, asparagus, oranges, cherries, to the rice. Let the rice mixture sit for at least 1 hour before use to absorb the liquid. Scoop the rice salad onto each lettuce leaf before serving. Sprinkle the zest over the filled leaves. Yield: 8 servings

Roasted Warm Beet Salad

2 lbs. fresh baby beets, sliced
1/2 C. balsamic vinegar
1 1/2 T. honey
1 T. olive oil
1/4 tsp. sea salt
1/8 tsp. pepper
2 C. quinoa or wild rice, cooked, if you are using the box do not use the seasoning package
Salad greens of choice, chopped

Preheat oven to 400°. Scrub beets and cut off the ends. Slice. Wear gloves to keep your fingers from turning red. Put beets in a casserole dish. Combine the dressing ingredients. Pour over the beets and bake at 400° for about an hour. Test for tenderness. Put warm quinoa or rice on a platter. Place beets on top. Pour the cooking juices which is the dressing over the beets. Surround the rim with chopped greens or just eat the beets!

Shredded Vegetable Salad
Kara Koprowski

Salad: Choose 5 vegetables, 1 C. of each
Bell pepper, all colors, halved and seeded
Yellow summer squash
Zuchini
Carrots
Beets, red, striped or golden, peeled
Napa cabbage
Cucumber
Radish

Vinaigrette Dressing:
1 garlic clove
1 tsp. mustard, Dijon or whole grain, not yellow
3/4 C. olive oil
6 T. balsamic vinegar
4 drops of Worcestershire sauce
4 T. Parmesan cheese
1/4 tsp. sugar
1/4 tsp. salt
1/4 tsp. paprika
freshly ground pepper
Optional nuts, toasted

Crush garlic clove with the side of a large knife. Place in a glass jar with a lid. Add rest of ingredients and shake well until dressing is thick and combined. Can add a few drops of water to thin if needed. Adjust salt and pepper to taste. Yield: 1 cup dressing

To Prepare the Salad: Shred all the vegetables using a food processor or box grater. When shredding beets put plastic bags over your hands to keep the dye from your hands. Choose 5 shredded vegetables, 1 cup of each. In a bowl toss using tongs one scoop of each vegetable with a few tablespoons of dressing. It makes a nice presentation to dress each vegetable separately. Place scoop of dressed vegetables on a bed of greens of choice. Can top with toasted nuts, such as almond or sunflower seeds, and sliced green onion. Yield: 5 servings

Wilted Kale Salad
Kara Koprowski

6 slices GF bacon
1 C. sweet onion, chopped
8 C. kale, thinly sliced, thick ribs removed
2 T. red wine vinegar
1/2 tsp. salt
1/2 tsp. pepper
1/2 C. goat cheese, crumbled

Chop and cook bacon until halfway cooked with some pink remaining on bacon. Add onion and cook an additional 5 to 7 minutes until onion is golden brown and bacon is fully cooked. In a large bowl, toss kale with vinegar, salt and pepper. Add bacon mixture and combine thoroughly. You can remove some of the bacon grease from pan if your bacon is very fatty but usually 6 strips will produce the right amount of fat to coat the kale. Kale will wilt slightly but not be completely soft. Top with goat cheese. Serve immediately. Yield: 4 cups

NOTES

Sweet Tooth

Angel Food Cake

1 2/3 C. egg whites, room temperature
1/2 C. potato starch
1/2 C. cornstarch
1 tsp. xanthan gum
3/4 C. white sugar
1/2 tsp. salt
1/2 tsp. cream of tartar
1 tsp. GF pure vanilla
1 tsp. GF almond
1 C. sifted white sugar

Preheat oven to 350°. Sift potato starch, cornstarch, gum and 3/4 cup sugar. Set aside. Put the egg whites in a mixing bowl with the extracts and cream of tartar. Beat on high until the whites are glossy and stiff. With the mixer going, sprinkle the remaining 1 cup sifted sugar. Turn the mixer on low and add the sifted dry ingredients. Pour batter into a 10 inch, ungreased tube pan. Bake at 350° for 60 minutes. Better to over bake this cake. When you take the cake from the oven turn it over on a long- necked bottle to cool. Yield: 8 to 10 slices.

Apple Cookies
Something different

1 large Granny Smith apple, chunked
1 C. unsalted whole almonds
1/2 C. unsweetened flaked coconut
1/4 C. dried apricots, chopped
2 tsp. canola oil
2 T. honey
1 tsp. GF pure vanilla
1 egg, beaten

Preheat oven to 350°. Peel apple and cut into chunks. Combine apple and all ingredients except egg together. Pulse in a food processor until coarsely ground. Add egg. Pulse to mix the egg into the rest of the ingredients. Shape into 1 inch balls. Drop onto greased, parchment paper lined cookie sheets. Space the cookie balls 2 inches apart. Flatten with a glass to 3/4 inch thickness. Keep glass bottom clean as you flatten. Bake 15 minutes or until light brown. Cool on cookie sheets for 5 minutes. Transfer cookies still on parchment to wire racks to cool completely. Yield: 12 cookies

Baked Apples, Crust-less

- 6 large apples, use firm apples, do not use Delicious or Golden Delicious
- 6 T. golden raisins, finely chopped
- 1/4 C. packed light brown sugar
- 1/4 C. unsalted butter, softened
- 1 tsp. ground cinnamon
- 3 T. GF oats
- 1/4 tsp. nutmeg
- 1/4 C. honey
- 1/2 C. apple cider
- 1 T. orange zest
- 1/4 C. pecans, chopped

Garnish:
- A dollop of sour cream or whipped cream

Peel the top half of the apples 1/2 way down the apple. Core out the center of the apple leaving at least 1/2 inch thick rim around the apple. Mix the dry filling ingredients together. Divide the mixture into 6 portions and press into the apple cavities. In a saucepan combine honey and cider. Heat enough to dissolve the honey. Pour over the stuffed apples and bake at 350° uncovered for about 40 minutes. Baste the apples, as they cook, with the pan juices. Let stand before serving. Pour the excess juice over them as they cool. Sprinkle the zest over each apple. Yield: 6 servings

Brownies from the Past

- 1 C. unsalted butter, softened
- 1/4 tsp. salt
- 2 C. sugar
- 4 eggs, room temperature
- 1 C. GF all purpose flour, see Two Flowers recipe
- 2 tsp. GF pure vanilla
- 3/4 C. cocoa
- 1/2 tsp. baking powder, see Two Flowers recipe
- 1/2 tsp. xanthan gum
- Nuts are optional
- Powdered sugar for dusting

Preheat oven to 350°. Do not use a mixer. Use a bowl and wooden spoon. Melt butter and stir in sugar, salt and vanilla. Add eggs and beat them into the egg mixture. Mix cocoa with baking powder, flour and gum. Add to mixing bowl and continue to mix until the ingredients are combined. Put a piece of parchment paper on the bottom of a 9 x 13 baking pan. Butter or spray the paper. Pour in the brownie batter and bake for 30 minutes. Test center with a toothpick to make sure it is done. Toothpick will come out clean when brownies are baked. Cut to desired size. Dust with powdered sugar.

Carrot Cake

- 3 C. pastry flour, see Two Flowers recipe
- 1 T. baking powder, see Two Flowers recipe
- 2 tsp. baking soda
- 1 tsp. salt
- 1 T. orange juice
- 1/2 tsp. orange rind, grated
- 1 tsp. cinnamon
- 1/2 tsp. nutmeg
- 2 C. sugar
- 1 1/2 C. canola oil
- 4 eggs, beaten
- 2 tsp. GF pure vanilla
- 2 C. carrots, peeled and shredded
- 1/2 C. golden raisins
- 1 C. walnuts, chopped
- 1 C. unsweetened flaked coconut
- Cream cheese frosting, see Two Flowers recipe

Preheat oven to 350°. Grease and prepare 2 9 inch cake pans. Cut a circle of wax paper or parchment paper for the bottom of each pan. Spray the bottom and the paper. Mix all dry ingredients together, except sugar. In another bowl combine sugar with oil and add eggs, orange juice, rind and vanilla. Add the dry ingredients to the liquid mix until totally incorporated. Fold in carrots, raisins, walnuts and coconut. Bake for 50 minutes. Remove cakes from the pans and peel off the paper from the cake bottoms. Frost with cream cheese frosting. Yield: 8 servings

Coconut Chocolate Balls

- 1 C. sweetened coconut, finely chopped
- 1/2 C. unsweetened coconut, finely chopped
- 1/3 C. sugar
- 1/8 tsp. salt
- 1/2 tsp. GF pure vanilla
- 1 tsp. GF pure almond
- 1 large egg white, beaten
- 1 tsp. water
- 18 chocolate chips

Preheat oven to 350°. Whisk both coconuts, sugar, salt. Mix in extracts with a wooden spoon. Add egg white and water. Mix until mixture holds together. Roll into tablespoon- sized balls and put chip in a small indent in the center. Re-roll to cover the chip. Place the cookies on a greased, parchment lined cookie sheet and bake for 12 minutes. Bottoms should be lightly browned so you can bake them up to 18 minutes if necessary. Put cookies on wire rack while still on cookie sheet to cool. Yield: 18 cookies

Chocolate Chippies

- 2 C. GF all purpose flour, see Two Flowers recipe
- 1 tsp. xanthan gum
- 2/3 tsp. baking soda
- 1/2 tsp. salt
- 1/4 C. unsalted butter, cut into chunks
- 1 1/4 C. light brown sugar, packed
- 1 egg
- 2 tsp. GF pure vanilla
- 1 1/4 C. semisweet chocolate chips

Preheat oven to 375°. Process flour, gum, baking soda and salt for 10 seconds in a food processor. Set aside. Process butter, sugar, egg and vanilla until light in color. Add flour mix and pulse until combined. Stir in chips. Refrigerate batter for 30 minutes. With a soup spoon mound each cookie, at least 2 inches apart on a greased, parchment lined cookie sheets. Pat down each cookie with a fork to flatten. Bake one pan at a time 8 minutes for a soft cookie. Bake 11 minutes for a browned cookie. Cool at least 10 minutes. Remove from pan onto a flat surface. They will firm up as they cool. Yield will depend on the size you choose.

Chocolate Cookies

- 1/2 C. + 3 T. cocoa powder
- 3 C. powdered sugar
- 1/8 tsp. salt
- 2 1/4 C. walnuts, chopped
- 4 large egg whites, room temperature
- 1 T. GF pure vanilla

Preheat oven to 350°. Combine cocoa, sugar, salt and walnuts in mixer. Mix on low speed for 1 minute. Slowly add egg whites and vanilla and mix for about 4 minutes more. Do not over mix or egg whites will be too thick. Scoop 1 tablespoon of mixture onto a greased, parchment lined cookie sheet leaving about 3 inches between cookies. Lower the oven from a 350° preheat to 320°. Bake for 15 minutes. Put the cookies, still on parchment paper, on wire rack to cool before removing them. Makes 12 4 inch cookies.

Chocolate Frosting
Pure heaven and you will never go back to frosting in a can

1 C. unsalted butter
2/3 C. cocoa
3 C. powdered sugar
1/3 C. whole milk or cream

1 tsp. GF pure vanilla
1/2 tsp. GF pure almond extract
Pinch of salt

Beat butter in an electric mixer until it becomes whipped. Mix sugar, milk, salt and extracts together and add to butter. Add sugar, a little at a time, and whip to a spreadable consistency. Leave out the cocoa for white frosting. This frosting is a Daisy and Rosie pick for the best ever!
Yield: 2 cups

Cheesecake Made Crustless

- 1 T. unsalted butter
- 4 C. cream cheese, room temperature
- 1 1/4 C. sugar
- 1 1/4 C. sour cream
- 6 eggs, room temperature
- 1 T. lemon juice
- 1 tsp. lemon zest
- 1 tsp. orange zest
- 1 T. GF pure vanilla

Topping:
- 3/4 C. sour cream
- 1/2 C. powdered sugar
- 1/4 tsp. GF pure vanilla

Preheat oven to 325°. Melt butter and brush the sides of a 9 inch springform pan. Prepare a roasting pan that will hold the springform pan. You will put boiling water in the pan so that it comes half way up the sides of the spring form pan. This baking method will help to keep cracking to a minimum. Beat the cream cheese and add the sugar. Continue beating until the mixture is light and fluffy. Scrape the bowl often to incorporate the cheese. Slowly add the sour cream and eggs one at a time. Add the vanilla and zests. Mix until incorporated. Pour batter into the spring form pan. Wrap foil around the outside of the pan to keep moisture out of the springform pan. Place the springform into the roasting pan with boiling water Bake for 1 1/4 hours at 325°. The center of the cake will be a bit loose. Cool the cake on a wire rack. Whisk the topping ingredients together and spread on the cooled cake. Return to oven for 5 minutes more at 325°. Turn off oven and let cheesecake sit in the oven for at least 1 more hour. Remove cake. Cool. Loosen sides. Refrigerate overnight. Bring back to room temperature before serving. Remove springform ring. Cut cake with a wet knife that you have dipped into hot water. Wipe knife after each slice. Yield: 8 to 10 slices

Chocolate Oatmeal No-Bake Drops
Quick and easy

1/2 stick unsalted butter, room temperature
1/4 C. whole milk
1 C. sugar
1/2 C. chocolate chips
1/2 tsp. GF pure vanilla
1/ 1/2 C. GF rolled oats
1/2 C. pecans, chopped
1 C. dried fruit of your choice

In a saucepan combine butter, milk and sugar over medium heat. Bring mixture to a boil and boil for 1 minute only. Stir in chips until melted. Add remaining ingredients and stir until mixed. Drop by the teaspoon onto a greased, parchment lined cookie sheet. Refrigerate 20 minutes. Store in container or freeze. Yield: 24 or more depending on how you size them

Chocolate Peanut Butter Cheesecake
Peanut butter and chocolate, what can be better?

Crust:
1 C. peanut butter, chunky
1 large egg, beaten
1 C. sugar
Filling:
32 oz. cream cheese, room temperature
3/4 C. sugar
1 tsp. GF pure vanilla
1/4 tsp. GF pure almond extract
1 C. sour cream
4 large eggs, beaten
2 C. creamy peanut butter
2 C. semisweet chocolate chips

Preheat oven to 350°. Spray a 9 inch springform pan with cooking spray. Make the crust by combining the peanut butter, egg and sugar. Spread mixture on the bottom of the springform pan. Bake for 8 minutes. Remove pan from the oven. In a mixing bowl beat the cream cheese, sugar and extracts until well combined. Add the sour cream. Add the eggs, one at a time until they are blended. Melt the peanut butter and the chips together over water. You may use the microwave but be careful as the chips will burn quickly. Stir the melted peanut butter/chip mixture into the batter. Pour the batter over the crust and bake for 50 minutes. Cool. Loosen the sides. Let the cheesecake set for at least 3 to 4 hours before cutting. Use a knife dipped in hot water to slice the cheesecake. Wipe the knife after each cut. Yield: 8 to 10 slices.

Chocolate Pie Filling

- 1 C. sugar
- 1/4 C. cornstarch
- 1/4 tsp. salt
- 3 C. whole milk
- 3 egg yolks + 1 whole egg
- 6 oz. GF bittersweet chocolate, chopped
- 2 T. unsalted butter
- 1 T. GF pure vanilla

Topping:
- 1 C. whipping cream
- 4 T. powdered sugar
- 1 tsp. GF pure vanilla

Whisk sugar, salt and cornstarch in a saucepan. Add egg yolks and whole egg. Cook over low heat stirring constantly. This will prevent the eggs from curdling. It will take about 8 to 10 minutes for mixture to come to a boil and thicken. Remove from heat and stir in chocolate. Stir until chocolate is totally melted. Add butter and vanilla. Cool and pour into a baked GF pie shell. Whip the cream with powdered sugar and vanilla. Add the powdered sugar a little at a time to the whipping cream. Spread on chocolate filling covering the chocolate to the edges. Yield: 6 + servings depending on your pie shell size.

Chocolate Pound Cake

- 1 1/2 C. GF all purpose flour, see Two Flowers recipe
- 1/2 tsp. xanthan gum
- 1/2 C. unsweetened cocoa
- 1/4 tsp. salt
- 2 oz. bittersweet chocolate
- 1 C. unsalted butter, softened
- 2 C. light brown sugar, packed
- 3 eggs
- 1 tsp. GF pure vanilla
- 1 C. sour cream

Preheat oven to 350°. Butter a 9 x 5 inch loaf pan. Sift flour, cocoa and salt and gum together. Melt the chocolate over boiling water, stirring. In a mixing bowl, beat the butter and brown sugar together until fluffy. Beat in the eggs one at a time. Add vanilla and chocolate. Stir. Add half the flour mixture then half of the sour cream. Repeat the additions ending with the remaining sour cream. Pour the batter into the loaf pan. Bake at 350° for 45 minutes to 1 hour. Test the center with a toothpick. It must come out clean to be fully baked. Yield: 8 slices

Chrusciki

Polish angel wing cookies, part of the Flowers' heritage

- 1 t. unsalted butter, melted
- 2 eggs + 5 egg yolks
- 1/4 C. sugar
- 3 T. sour cream
- 2 tsp. salt
- 1 tsp. pure lemon extract
- 1 tsp. lemon peel, grated
- 1 tsp. GF pure vanilla
- 1 tsp. white vinegar
- 1 T. rum or brandy
- 2 to 3 C. GF all purpose flour plus extra for dusting, see Two Flowers recipe
- 3/4 tsp. xanthan gum
- Vegetable oil for frying
- Powdered sugar for dusting

In a mixing bowl add melted butter, eggs, egg yolks, sugar, sour cream, salt, extracts, vinegar, and rum. Beat mixture for about 3 minutes until pale in color. Whisk the flour and gum together. Put mixer on low and gradually add the flour mixture to the egg mixture until a stiff dough is formed. Put dough on a GF floured board and knead. If it seems too sticky keep adding a bit more flour. When a nice dough ball results after kneading divide it in half. Wrap each half in plastic wrap and place on the counter to rest for 30 minutes. Work with one piece of dough at a time and roll the dough on a GF floured surface into a thin, 1/16 th. inch, rectangle. With a pastry cutter or another straight edge, cut the dough into 5 inch by 2 inch strips. Lay strips out. Cut a small slit, about 1 inch wide in the middle of each strip. Pull one end through the slit to form a bow tie shape. Cover the finished strips with a damp cloth. Heat shortening to 375° and drop a few bow ties at a time into the oil. Fry until they are golden brown. Drain on paper towels. Dust with powdered sugar. Before serving, re-dust with sugar. You can re-crisp by putting wings into a 350° oven for a few minutes. Yield: about 6 dozen

Cinnamon and Spice Caramel Popcorn
Kara Koprowski different twist to popcorn

10 C. air popped popcorn which is 1/3 cup of popcorn kernels. Do not use more than 1/3 cup, see Two Flowers recipe for microwaved popcorn
1 tsp. baking soda
1 tsp. cinnamon
1 tsp. ginger
1 tsp. nutmeg
1 C. light brown sugar
1/4 C. sugar
1/3 C. light corn syrup
1/3 C. water
3 T. unsalted butter
1 tsp. salt
1 tsp. GF pure vanilla

Place popped popcorn on a large baking sheet lined with parchment paper. In a small bowl, stir together baking soda, cinnamon, ginger, and nutmeg. Set aside. Cook sugars, corn syrup, water and butter in a medium sized thick bottomed saucepan over medium heat until the temperature reaches 300° hard crack stage. It is best to use a candy thermometer but should take 6 to 8 minutes. Do not go past 300° or the mixture will burn. Stir occasionally. Remove from heat and add spice mixture, salt and vanilla. Working quickly, pour mixture over popcorn. Can use silicone spatulas to distribute the caramel throughout. Let cool and gently break apart. Store in an airtight container at room temperature. Makes about 11 1 cup servings. NOTE: Can also add 1 cup of semi-sweet chocolate chips and/or 1/2 cup of dried fruit such as cherries or cranberries after caramel is poured over the popcorn or after the mixture is cooled.

Cream Cheese Frosting

16 oz. softened cream cheese
1/2 C. unsalted butter
1/4 tsp. salt
2 C. powdered sugar
1 tsp. GF pure vanilla
1/2 tsp. orange rind, grated

In a mixer, beat cream cheese with butter and salt. Add powdered sugar a little at a time until you have obtained a spreadable frosting. Add vanilla and orange rind at the end.

Cream Puffs

1 C. water
1/2 C. unsalted butter
1/3 C. potato starch
2/3 C. rice flour
1/2 tsp. salt
1 T. sugar
4 eggs, room temperature

Filling:
2 C. heavy cream, whipped
2 T. powdered sugar
1/2 tsp. GF pure vanilla
Glaze:
2 C. warm heavy cream or milk
1 C. semisweet chocolate chips
Splash of vanilla or brewed coffee

Preheat oven to 450°. Line a cookie sheet with parchment paper. Spray the paper. Combine water and butter in a saucepan. Bring to a boil. Stir in all the dry ingredients with a wooden spoon until mixture leaves the side of the pan. Add 1 egg at a time beating vigorously. You can use a hand mixer to make this easier. Remove from heat. Drop tablespoons of batter in 2 inch rounds on the cookie sheet. This will make large puffs. Drop by teaspoons to make appetizer sized puffs. Bake for 20 minutes in a 450° oven. Lower heat to 350° and bake 20 minutes more. Prick the tops to let the steam out. Cool. Mix the 3 filling ingredients to fill puffs. Warm cream on the stove and add chocolate chips to melt. Add flavoring. Cool until spreadable. Glaze the top of each puff. Store the cream puffs unfilled in a vented container. Crisp them up in a 350° oven before filling for just a few minutes.

Cut-Out Sugar Cookies
Kara Koprowski

Cookies:
1 C. white rice flour
3/4 C. tapioca flour
1/4 tsp. salt
1/2 tsp. baking powder, see Two Flowers recipe
1/2 C. unsalted butter, softened
3/4 C. sugar
1 egg
1 tsp. GF pure vanilla
Frosting:
2 C. powdered sugar, sifted
1/2 C. unsalted butter, softened
1/2 tsp. GF pure vanilla
1 T. milk

Preheat oven to 350°. Line two cookie sheets with parchment paper. In a bowl, whisk flours, salt and baking powder. In a medium mixing bowl, cream butter and add sugar. Beat until fluffy. Add egg and vanilla. Add flour mixture and beat until smooth. Divide dough in half and wrap in plastic wrap. Flatten to a disk shape and refrigerate for one hour. After one hour, remove dough and roll dough to a 1/4 inch thickness using tapioca flour or cornstarch on your rolling surface. Cut cookies with a cookie cutter. Dip the cutter in GF flour before cutting. It will make it easier for cut-outs. Transfer to cookie sheets and place in the refrigerator for 15 minutes. Bake cookies for 8 to 10 minutes. Let cool before transferring to a wire rack.

To make frosting, cream butter using electric mixer until smooth. Gradually beat in sugar, then add vanilla and milk. Beat on high speed until frosting is smooth.

Options: For the holidays can cut cookies into candy-cane shape and use chopped peppermint candy canes on top of frosting. Can top with sanding sugar or other chopped candies of choice.

Date Bars

Crust:
- 2 C. GF oats
- 3/4 C. GF all purpose flour, see Two Flowers recipe
- 1/4 C. almond flour
- 1/4 tsp. xanthan gum
- 1 C. packed light brown sugar
- 1 tsp. baking soda
- 3/4 C. unsalted butter, melted

Filling:
- 2 1/2 C. dates, chopped and pitted
- 3/4 C. water
- 1 1/2 tsp. lemon juice
- 1/3 C. brown sugar

Preheat oven to 350°. Grease a 9 inch baking pan. Stir the oats, flours, baking soda, and sugar together in a bowl. Add the melted butter and stir until mixture is moist and crumbly. Press 1/2 the oat mixture in the bottom of the pan. Prepare filling by combining all ingredients in a saucepan. Cook until the mixture thickens, about 5 to 10 minutes. Cool. Spread the date mixture on top of prepared crust and sprinkle the remaining oat mixture on top. Bake in 350° oven for 40 minutes. Cool. Cut into bars.

Double Chocolate Truffles
Kara Koprowski

- 12 oz. semisweet chocolate, coarsely chopped
- 12 oz. bittersweet chocolate, coarsely chopped
- 1 C. whipping cream
- 4 T. unsalted butter
- 1 T. GF pure vanilla

Chocolate Coating:
- 12 oz. semisweet chocolate, chips or coarsely chopped chocolate
- 1 T. unsalted butter

Combine chocolate in a large mixing bowl. In a heavy saucepan, heat cream, butter and vanilla until hot and bubbling. Pour over chocolate. Let stand 1 minute and whisk until smooth. Chill until firm, about an hour. Using a 1 tablespoon cookie scoop, roll the dough in your palms to form a smooth ball. Place balls on a foil or parchment lined cookie sheet. Freeze until firm. Melt remaining 12 ounces of chocolate and butter in a small narrow pot or mini crock pot. Dip truffles one at a time in melted chocolate. Using a tooth pick helps. After truffles are dipped, you can swirl a small amount of melted chocolate over the top to cover the hole where the toothpick was used. Place on prepared sheet and sprinkle with coarse sea salt, chopped nuts or other coatings if desired before chocolate sets. Store in an airtight container. Makes approximately 30 truffles.

Dream Bars

- 1/2 C. unsalted butter
- 1 1/2 C. GF graham crackers or GF cookies
- 1 C. GF semisweet chocolate chips
- 1 C. GF butterscotch chips
- 1 C. walnuts, pecans or peanuts, chopped
- 1 14 oz. can sweetened condensed milk
- 1/2 tsp. GF pure vanilla
- 1 1/3 C. sweetened flaked coconut

Preheat oven to 350°. In a food processor, process crackers or cookies into a fine grind. Melt the butter in the bottom of a 9 x 13 baking pan. Sprinkle crumbs over the butter. This will be the first layer. In a bowl add vanilla to the condensed milk and stir well. Set aside. Continue to sprinkle remaining ingredients layer by layer as they are listed. Pour the milk mixture over all the layers and top with coconut. Bake for 20 to 25 minutes until light brown. Cool and cut into desired squares.

Donuts

- 2 C. GF all purpose flour, see Two Flowerss recipe
- 1/2 C. sugar
- 1 tsp. salt
- 1 T. baking powder, see Two Flowers recipe
- 1/2 tsp. xanthan gum
- 1 tsp. salt
- 1 tsp. cinnamon
- 1 tsp. nutmeg
- 5 T. unsalted butter
- 3/4 C. milk
- 1 beaten egg
- Canola oil for frying

Glaze:
- 1/4 C. milk
- 1 tsp. GF pure vanilla
- 2 C. powdered sugar

Sift together all dry ingredients. Cut in butter with a pastry cutter or fork until crumbly. Stir in milk and egg. Knead dough and roll out to 1/2 inch thickness. Use more GF flour for the surface and the rolling pin. Use a cookie cutter or glass dipped in flour for the cutting of the donut round. Drop the donut into 375° oil for about 3 minutes. Turn to brown the other side. Drain on a paper towel and top with glaze.

Glaze: Mix milk in saucepan and heat until warm. Whisk in sugar and continue to heat until slightly melted. Dip the doughnut in the warm glaze one at a time. Cool on a wire rack. Recipe can be used in an electric donut maker.

Festive Fudge
Quick and easy

3 C. semisweet chocolate chips
1 can sweetened condensed milk, not evaporated
1 C. walnuts or pecans, chopped, optional
1 1/2 tsp. GF pure vanilla
1/8 tsp. salt

In a heavy saucepan over low heat, melt chocolate chips with condensed milk and salt until mixture is smooth and glossy. Add vanilla. Remove from heat and stir in nuts if desired. Spread evenly on a wax paper lined 8 inch square pan. Chill at least 2 hours until firm. Turn fudge upside down onto a cutting board and peel off wax paper. Cut into squares. Store in an airtight container and keep refrigerated.

Marshmallow Fudge: Add 2 tablespoons unsalted melted butter to melted fudge mixture. Remove from heat and fold in 2 cups miniature marshmallows.

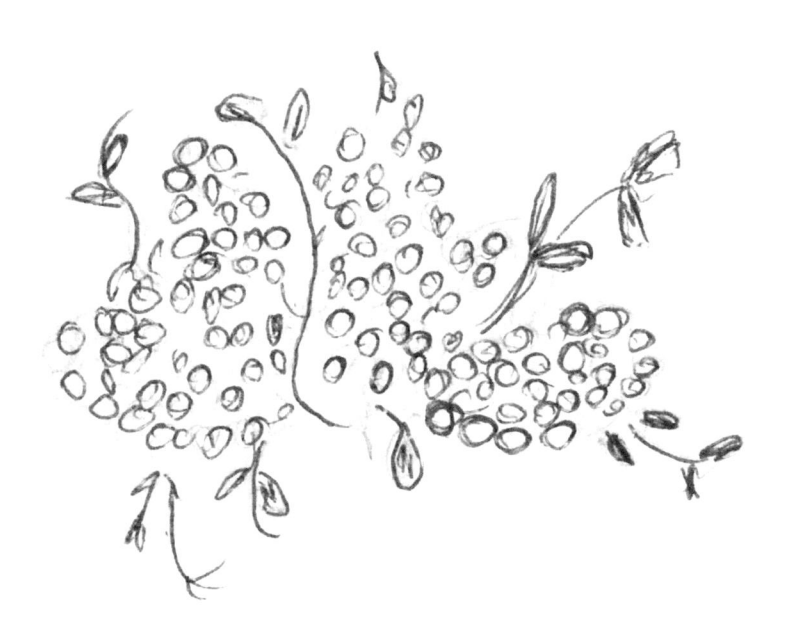

Fresh Peach Cobbler

10 fresh peaches, peeled and sliced
1/2 C. sugar
1 T. of the brown rice mixture from below
Brown Rice Flour Mix:
1 C. brown rice flour
1/3 C. potato starch
1/4 C. tapioca starch
Cobbler Topping:
1 C. brown rice flour mix
3 tsp. sugar
1 tsp. baking powder, see Two Flowers recipe
1/4 tsp. xanthan gum
1/4 tsp. baking soda
1/4 tsp. salt
1 tsp. cinnamon
1/4 C. unsalted butter, broken into small pieces
1/2 C. buttermilk
1/2 tsp. GF pure vanilla
2 T. unsalted butter, melted
2 T. brown sugar
Addition:
Ice cream or whipped cream

Preheat oven t0 350°. Peel peaches by dropping them in boiling water for a few minutes. The skins will come off easily. Pit and slice peaches. Combine sliced peaches with 1/2 cup sugar and 1 tablespoon flour mix. Pour mixture into a 9 x 13 buttered dish. Whisk flour mix, sugar, gum, baking soda, powder, salt, and cinnamon together. Put in chunks of butter and with a pastry cutter or with your hands crumble the mixture until it is fine. Add the buttermilk and vanilla to flour mixture. Pour over the peaches. Melt 2 tablespoons butter and pour over the mix. Sprinkle brown sugar evenly on top. Bake 40 minutes uncovered. Serve with ice cream or whipped cream with a little cinnamon or nutmeg mixed in the whipping cream. Yield: 8 servings

Flourless Chocolate Cake

1 1/2 C. semisweet chocolate, chopped
1/2 C. unsalted butter
1/4 tsp. salt
6 large eggs, beaten
1 1/2 C. sugar
1 tsp. GF pure vanilla
6 T. rum
Cocoa for dusting
Whipped cream for topping

Preheat oven to 325°. In the microwave, melt chocolate with butter and salt. Whip eggs and vanilla with sugar until fluffy. Fold melted chocolate mixture into egg mixture. Pour batter into a buttered 9 inch springform pan. Wrap the pan with foil to keep batter from dripping. Bake 1 1/2 hours. Cool on a wire rack. Dust with either powdered sugar or cocoa. Serve with a dollop of whipped cream. Yield: 8 + servings

Fruity Macaroons

1 14 oz. can sweetened condensed milk
1/2 tsp. GF pure vanilla
1 C. pecans, chopped
1 C. almonds, slivered
2 C. sweetened coconut
1/4 C. dried cherries or cranberries, chopped
1/4 C. dried apricots, chopped
3 large egg whites
1/4 tsp. salt
3/4 C. melted chocolate chips for drizzle
Pure cooking spray

Preheat oven to 325°. Line cookie sheets with parchment paper and spray with cooking spray. Mix milk with extracts. Pulse nuts in the food processor until it resembles small pieces. Stir in all other ingredients except whites. Beat egg whites until soft peaks form. Fold 1/2 cup of egg whites into coconut mixture. Add remaining egg whites, folding them into coconut mixture. Drop by the teaspoon onto the cookie sheet and bake until golden, 20 minutes. Let cool 30 minutes. Melt the chips over hot water rather than in a microwave. They are less likely to burn. Drizzle melted chocolate over the top of each cookie. Yield: 50 cookies.

Granola Bar on the Go

3/4 C. honey
3/4 C. creamy GF peanut butter, see Two Flowers recipe
1 tsp. GF pure vanilla
1 C. semisweet chocolate chips
1/2 C. raw or roasted almonds, whole or pieces
1/2 C. roasted cashews, whole or pieces
2 C. GF oats
2 C. GF crispy rice cereal
1/3 C. ground flax seed
1/2 C. sweetened flaked coconut
1 C. sunflower seeds or pepitas, pumpkin seeds
1 C. dried chopped fruit of choice such as raisins, cherries, blueberries, apricots. etc.

Preheat oven to 350°. Lightly grease a 10 x 15 jelly roll pan. In a large mixing bowl, combine all dry ingredients. In a separate bowl, mix honey, peanut butter and vanilla together. Mix wet ingredients into dry ingredients. It is easier to oil your hands and then use your hands. Spread the mixture evenly in the prepared pan and bake 18 to 20 minutes. Check granola at 18 minutes as you do not want to over bake. Granola will harden as it cools. Cool on a wire rack and cut into bars. Let bars cool completely in pan before removing. Store in an airtight container.

Gumdrops
Why make gum drops? Try them!

3 envelopes unflavored gelatin
1 C. water
1/4 tsp. peppermint extract
Pure green, yellow, and red food coloring

Soften gelatin in 1/2 cup water about 3 to 5 minutes. In a saucepan bring sugar and remaining water to a boil, stirring constantly. Add gelatin. Simmer and stir for an additional 5 minutes. Remove from heat and stir in peppermint. Divide mixture into 3 bowls. Add a few drops of each food color to each bowl. Stir and pour each mixture into greased loaf pans. Chill until firm in the refrigerator. Loosen from pan and cut into small cubes. Roll the cubes into sugar. Let stand at room temperature, uncovered, for 4 to 5 hours. This will help them dry out. Keep turning the cubes in the sugar to coat. When the sides are dry put into a covered container and chill. Yield: about 1 lb.

Ice Cream in the Food Processor
Quick, easy and delicious! No ice cream maker needed. Anita Krotine

1 C. whipping cream	1/2 C. sugar
12 oz. frozen whole strawberries or other frozen fruit without sauce	2 pasteurized eggs or the equivalent of liquid eggs
	1 tsp. GF pure vanilla

In food processor pour in the whipping cream and start to process. Add sugar, eggs, vanilla as it is whipping. Add fruit pieces one at a time. It will become ice cream at the end of the processing. Store in the freezer. If you use sweetened fruit omit the sugar. Yield: 3 to 4 servings

Lemon Angel Pie
A meringue shell makes this dessert elegant

Shell:
3 egg whites, room temperature
1/4 tsp. cream of tartar
1/4 tsp. salt
3/4 C. sugar
1 tsp. GF pure vanilla
Filling:
3 egg yolks
3/4 C. sugar
1/2 C. fresh lemon juice
2 T. lemon peel, grated
1/8 tsp. salt
1/2 pt. whipping cream
1/3 C. sugar
1 tsp. GF pure vanilla
Lemon slices and mint for garnish

Preheat oven to 350°. Beat egg whites with cream of tartar until foamy. Add salt. On high speed add sugar a little at a time to make a shiny mixture. Add vanilla. Grease a 9 inch pie pan. Coat the sides of the pan with the meringue. Bake meringue for at least an hour. Turn off oven but leave it in the oven with the door open to dry it out. Filling: Beat yolks in top of double boiler until thick. Gradually beat in 3/4 cup sugar. Add all other ingredients except vanilla and mix well. Stir well over simmering water until mixture thickens. Beat whipped cream with 1/3 cup sugar and vanilla. Fold whipped cream into lemon mixture and spread into cooled shell. Can freeze this pie. If frozen, thaw 15 minutes before slicing. Garnish with lemon slices and mint. Yield: 6 to 8 slices

Luscious Lemon Bars

Crust:
1 C. unsalted butter
1/2 C. sugar
2 C. all purpose flour mix
see Two Flowers recipe
1/2 tsp. xanthan gum
1/8 tsp. salt
GF pure cooking spray

Filling:
6 eggs
2 1/2 C. sugar
1 C. fresh lemon juice
2 T. lemon zest
1 C. all purpose flour, see
  Two Flowers recipe
1/2 tsp. baking powder, see
  Two Flowers recipe
Powdered sugar for dusting

Preheat oven to 350°. Line a 9 x 13 baking pan with parchment paper. Spray the paper with cooking spray. Make sure the paper comes up on all four sides. This will make the bars easier to remove from the pan. Combine crust ingredients in a food processor until a dough ball forms. Pat the dough down in baking pan with your hands. Smooth the dough evenly over the surface. Bake for 20 minutes at 350°. Meanwhile prepare the filling. In the food processor or mixer combine eggs, sugar, zest and juice until the mixture is foamy. Gradually add the flour. Make sure it is all incorporated. Pour over the crust and bake for 30 minutes more. Cool and lift out the pan of bars. Cut into desired size. Be sure and peel off the parchment paper. Dust with powdered sugar. Yield: 24 smaller sized bars

Melt-in-Your Mouth Lemon Drops

1 C. brown rice flour
1/3 C. potato starch
2 1/2 T. tapioca flour
1/4 tsp. xanthan gum
1/2 C. cornstarch
1/4 C. + 2 T. almond flour
2 sticks unsalted butter, softened
1/2 C. powdered sugar
2 T. lemon juice
2 tsp. lemon zest, grated
1/2 tsp. lemon extract
GF pure cooking spray

Preheat oven to 350°. Sift all dry ingredients except almond flour. Whisk in almond flour. In an electric mixer combine butter and 1/2 cup powdered sugar on high speed until mixture is light and fluffy. Add the 3 lemon ingredients. Beat until combined. Add flour and beat until smooth. Chill dough for several hours. Line a cookie sheet with parchment paper. Spray with cooking spray. Make teaspoon-sized balls and space them 1 inch apart. Bake for 15 minutes. Immediately dust with extra powdered sugar. Re-dust before serving. Yield: 36 to 42 cookies

Minty Chocolate Loaf Cake

8 oz. semisweet chocolate, chopped
8 T. unsalted butter, chopped
1/4 C. heavy cream
3 eggs
2 T. sugar
1/2 tsp. peppermint extract
Garnish:
1 tsp. cocoa
1 C. whipped cream, whipped
fresh mint leaves
GF pure cooking spray

Preheat oven to 350°. Fill a deep pan half way up with water. Put the pan into the oven to heat the water. With cooking spray coat a 9 x 5 loaf pan. Cut a piece of parchment paper to fit the bottom and the sides of the loaf pan. Spray the paper with cooking spray. Melt the chocolate and butter over low gently simmering water. When melted, remove from heat and cool. Whip the cream with an electric mixer. You need to whip the cream into soft peaks. In another bowl of the mixer whip up the eggs and sugar until they are light lemon colored and fluffy. Fold half of the chocolate mixture into the egg mixture. Fold well. Continue folding in the chocolate until it is all incorporated. Gently whisk in the whipped cream and peppermint extract. In the loaf pan spread the batter, evenly. Reduce oven temperature to 325°. Put the loaf pan into the roasting pan of water. Bake batter for 25 minutes or until the sides loosen. Remove the loaf pan from the water and cool. When cooled invert the loaf cake onto a plate and carefully remove the paper. Dust the torte with the cocoa and decorate with mint and whipped cream. Yield: 6 to 8 slices

Nut and Honey Bars

Crust:
1/2 C. whole almonds
1/2 C. sugar
2 1/2 C. GF all purpose flour, see Two Flowers recipe
1/2 tsp. xanthan gum
1/2 tsp. baking powder, see Two Flowers recipe
1/2 tsp. salt
12 T. unsalted butter, cold
1 large egg, beaten
GF pure cooking spray

Topping:
3/4 C. packed brown sugar
6 T. unsalted butter
1/3 C. honey
1/2 tsp. salt
2 T. heavy cream
3 C. GF mixed nuts

Preheat oven to 350°. Spray a 9 x 13 pan with cooking spray. Line the bottom of the pan with parchment paper and spray the paper. Process the almonds to a fine grind with the sugar. Add the flour, baking powder and salt. Blend. Add the butter pieces and blend to form small peas. Add the egg. Now you will have a dough. Press the dough into the bottom of the pan. Go up the side of the pan about 1/4 inch to form a nice bottom crust. Prick the crust with a fork. Bake for 15 minutes in a 350° oven.

Topping:
In a sauce pan bring brown sugar, butter, honey and salt to a boil, stirring often. Slowly add cream and bring back to a boil. Add nuts and stir to coat. Pour nut mixture evenly over the crust. Put back into the oven for 20 minutes more. Let cool. Run a knife around the edges and cool completely. Turn pan over and peel off the paper. Turn it right side up and cut into bars.

Oatmeal Raisin Cookies

- 1/2 C. butter
- 1/2 C. sugar
- 1/2 C. brown sugar, packed
- 1 egg
- 1 egg white
- 1/2 tsp. vanilla
- 1 1/2 C. GF all purpose flour, see Two Flowers recipe
- 1/2 tsp. baking soda
- 1 tsp. baking powder
- 1/4 tsp. salt
- 1 tsp. cinnamon
- 1 tsp. xanthan gum
- 1 1/2 C. GF oats
- 1/2 C. raisins

Preheat oven to 350°. Cream sugars with butter until fluffy. Add egg and white one at a time. Add vanilla. In another bowl combine all the dry ingredients. Stir dry ingredients into creamed ingredients. Add oats and raisins and mix well.

Chill dough for a few hours. With greased hands make a tablespoon sized ball. Place the balls 2 inches apart on a greased, parchment lined cookie sheet. Bake in a 350° oven for 10 minutes. Yield: 36 cookies

Oatmeal Snack Cake

Cake:
- 1 C. GF oatmeal
- 1 1/3 C. boiling water
- 1/2 C. unsalted butter
- 3/4 C. sugar
- 3/4 C. brown sugar
- 2 eggs
- 1 1/3 C. GF all purpose flour, see Two Flowers recipe
- 1/2 tsp. xanthan gum
- 1 tsp. baking soda
- 1 tsp. salt
- 1 tsp. cinnamon
- 1/4 tsp. cloves
- 1/4 tsp. nutmeg
- 1 tsp. GF pure vanilla
- 1/2 C. pecans, chopped

Broiled Frosting:
- 1 1/2 C. packed light brown sugar
- 6 T. unsalted butter, melted and cooled
- 1/4 C. cream
- 1/2 C. unsweetened coconut
- 1/2 C. pecans, chopped

Preheat 325°. Make a foil sling inside the 9 x 13 pan so that you have an overlap of foil on all 4 sides. This way you will be able to lift out the cake to put on a cake plate. Grease the pan. In a bowl combine water and oats until the water is fully absorbed. Whisk all the dry ingredients with spices. Set aside. In the bowl of the mixer beat butter and sugars until fluffy. Add eggs and vanilla. Beat until incorporated. Add flour mixture a little at a time. Add soaked oatmeal to batter. Stir the batter and pour into the prepared pan. Run a knife through the batter in the pan to release the air bubbles. Bake 35 to 40 minutes.

Frosting: Beat butter and milk together with the brown sugar. Stir in pecans and coconut. Spread frosting over the cooled cake and put under the broiler for a few minutes to brown the frosting. Yield: 6 to 8 servings

Peanut Butter Cookies
5 ingredients, that's it

1 C. sugar
1 egg
1 tsp. baking soda
1 C. peanut butter, can use chunky or smooth
1 tsp. GF pure vanilla

Preheat oven to 350°. Cream sugar and egg together. Add soda and peanut butter and vanilla. Mix well. Form into the size cookie you want to have and slightly flatten it into shape with a fork. Bake on an ungreased cookie sheet for 10 to 15 minutes. Cool on a wire rack. You can also dip these cookies in melted chocolate. Yield: 1 dozen

Peanut Butter Haystacks
A no-bake quick treat

2 C. peanut butter chips
1 C. semisweet chocolate chips
1 1/2 C. GF salted peanuts, not dry roasted
1 C. GF traditional style potato chips, crushed

Melt peanut butter and chocolate chips in a saucepan over low heat. Stir until smooth. Stir in peanuts and crushed potato chips. Drop onto waxed paper in small clumps. Cool in refrigerator. Yield: 36 pieces.

Pie Crust

- 1/4 C. GF all purpose flour, see Two Flowers recipe
- 1 T. sugar
- 1/2 tsp. xanthan gum
- 1/4 tsp. sea salt
- 1/4 C. unsalted butter, frozen if possible
- 1/4 C. GF shortening, cold
- 1 large egg, cold
- 3 T. ice water
- 1/4 tsp. cider vinegar
- 9" pie plate

Combine dry ingredients in a food processor. Add slices of frozen butter and cold shortening to flour mixture. Mix in egg, vinegar and ice water. Add the ice water little by little to make the dough rollable using the food processor on pulse. Remove from processor and shape pastry into 2 discs and wrap in plastic wrap. Chill wrapped discs for at least 1 hour. Remove from refrigerator, remove plastic wrap and place between 2 pieces of wax paper or plastic wrap. Roll into a 12 inch circle. Take wax paper off the top, turn it over into a 9 inch pie plate. For a pre-baked crust, prick bottom of crust with a fork and bake at 475° for 8 to 10 minutes. Cool. Fill with your choice of filling. Otherwise, proceed with your favorite pie recipe. Yield: 2 pie crusts

Pineapple Upside-Down Cake

Topping:

1/4 C. softened unsalted butter
3/4 C. packed light brown sugar
1/4 tsp. nutmeg
1/4 tsp. cinnamon
1/2 tsp. GF pure vanilla
6 slices fresh pineapple
Cake:
3/4 C. white rice four
3/8 C. GF all purpose flour,
see Two Flowers recipe

1/2 tsp. salt
1/2 tsp. baking soda
1 1/2 tsp. baking powder,
see Two Flowers recipe
1/2 tsp. xanthan gum
2 eggs, beaten
1 C. white sugar
1/3 C. GF mayonnaise,
see Two Flowers recipe
1/2 C. milk
1 tsp. pure vanilla

Use sweet fresh cherries for the centers of the pineapple if you want the 50's look. Preheat oven to 350*. In an 8 inch round baking pan melt 2 tablespoons of butter. Add brown sugar, spices and vanilla. Bring mixture to a boil and stir to dissolve the sugar. Place the pineapple rings in the mixture and cook them until they are tender. Remove the rings to another pan. Continue to cook the sugar mixture for an additional 5 minutes. The mixture will be golden brown. Set aside. In a mixing bowl combine all the dry ingredients and stir well. Add the eggs, mayonnaise, milk and vanilla and mix well. Into the bottom of an 8 inch pan pour the sugar mixture. Add the pineapple rings in a circle with the cherries in the center. Evenly spread the batter over the pineapple rings. Bake in a 350* oven for about 30 minutes. Make sure the toothpick comes out clean when testing the cake. Cool for 20 minutes and invert over a serving dish. This will allow the sugar to coat the cake. You will not go back to canned rings again. Yield: 6-8 servings

Pistachio Dacquoise (Meringue)
Company is coming...

Shell:
1 C. chopped pistachio nuts
1/2 C. powdered sugar
6 egg whites
1 C. sugar
1/4 tsp. salt
1/8 tsp. cream of tartar
2 C. fresh raspberries or any berries

Pastry Filling:
1/2 C. sugar
2 large egg yolks
1/4 tsp. salt
1/4 C. cornstarch
2 C. milk
1 1/2 C. whipping cream

Preheat oven to 200°. On a large sheet of parchment paper trace 3 8 inch round circles. In a bowl add nuts to the powdered sugar. Place sugar, cream of tartar and salt in a bowl over warm water and proceed to dissolve the sugar mixture with a whisk. Add the egg whites and continue to whisk. You want to warm up the egg whites. This will take a few minutes. When sugar mixture is dissolved transfer to a mixing bowl. Beat with the whisk attachment until soft, glossy peaks form. Gently fold in the nut/powdered sugar mixture. Divide the meringue mixture evenly among the 3 circles. Bake for 1 to 2 hours until the meringue is dry and stiff. The circles will remove quite easily from the paper. Let them remain in oven that is turned off. Process 3/4 cup of the berries to form a puree. Pour through a strainer and throw away the seeds.

Pastry Cream Filling:
Whisk the 1/4 cup sugar, yolks and salt in a bowl. Add cornstarch, a little at a time. Bring milk and remaining sugar to a simmer in a saucepan. Add the milk mixture to the yolk mixture a little at a time, whisking continually. Add the incorporated mixture to the saucepan and bring back to a boil. Cook until thickened. Strain out any solids and refrigerate in a bowl with plastic wrap over the cream to prevent a film from forming. Before serving whip the cream and gently fold it into the pastry cream. Put a meringue circle on a serving plate and cover with the pastry filling. Repeat. End with a pastry cream layer. Freeze for 1 to 2 hours before serving. You do not want it to be frozen solid but it will help with the cutting. Pour the puree over the top and garnish with berries and whipped cream. Cut with a serrated knife. Yield: 8 to 12 servings

Polish Cream Cheese Cookies
Jean Koprowski

8 oz. cold cream cheese
1 C. unsalted butter
1 C. white rice flour
1 C. almond flour
1 tsp. xanthan gum

1 C. dried apricots
3 C. water
1/4 C. sugar
1 T. fresh lemon juice
Powdered sugar to dust cookies

Preheat oven to 350°. In the food processor process the cream cheese, butter, 2 flours and gum. Process until ingredients form a ball. Wrap the dough in plastic wrap and refrigerate. Meanwhile cover the apricots with water and bring them to a boil. Simmer uncovered for about 45 minutes. Add water if necessary to keep the apricots covered with water. When softened, drain. Place the apricots in the food processor and puree with the lemon juice and sugar. Remove dough from the refrigerator. Cut the ball of dough into 4 parts. Roll out each part between 2 sheets of wax paper to a 1/8 inch thickness. Cut the dough with a pastry cutter or knife into 2 inch squares. Place a dab of the filling in the center of each square. Fold over the corner to form a triangle. Seal the edges with the tines of the fork to give it a decorative edge. Place the cookies on a greased, parchment lined cookie sheet a few inches apart and bake for 12 minutes. Keep an eye on them as GF flour browns quicker than wheat flour. When cool dust with powdered sugar.
Yield: 3 dozen cookies

Polish Custard Cake
Ever so simple!

- 1/2 C. sugar
- 1 tsp. GF pure vanilla
- 2 T. potato starch
- 1 T. grated lemon zest + 1 T. fresh lemon juice
- 16 oz. full fat cottage cheese, small curd
- 4 large eggs, separated
- 1 C. sour cream
- 1/4 tsp. sea salt

Topping:
- 1/4 C. sour cream
- 2 T. sugar
- 1/2 tsp. GF pure vanilla

Preheat oven to 325°. Butter an 8 inch round or square pan. Separate eggs into two bowls and keep them at room temperature. Whisk yolks and stir in 1 tablespoon sour cream. Add sugar, potato starch, lemon juice and zest to yolks. Drain and press all liquid out of cottage cheese using a fine mesh strainer. (Can use the back of a wooden spoon to press the liquid out). Add cottage cheese to yolk mixture and stir until blended. Beat egg whites until soft peaks form. Fold 1/4 of the egg whites to cheese mixture. Completely fold in remaining egg whites until incorporated into batter. Pour batter into cake pan and bake for 40 minutes. Remove from oven and spread topping on and bake 5 minutes more until topping sets. This custard cake can be eaten without the topping if desired. Raisins or nuts can be added to cheese mixture if desired. Yield: 8 to 10 slices

Rice Pudding

Gladys Nosse - the golden raisins and dried apricots make a difference in this classic pudding

1 C. cooked rice
2 1/2 C. whole milk
4 large beaten eggs
1/2 C. sugar
1/2 C. golden raisins
1/2 C. dried apricots, slivered

1 tsp. GF pure vanilla
1/2 tsp. GF pure almond extract
1/4 tsp. sea salt
1/2 tsp. cinnamon
1/4 tsp. nutmeg

Preheat oven to 325°. Mix eggs, milk and sugar. Add extracts and seasonings. Add rice. Mix in raisins and apricots. Grease a 9 inch square pan and pour mixture into it. Fill a roasting pan with boiling water, high enough to surround the rice pudding pan half way up. Place the pudding pan into it. This is called a water bath and it will keep pudding moist. Bake for 1 hour, covered. Test to see if it is golden and firm. If not, bake another 10 to 20 minutes. Yield: 8 servings

Simply Chocolate Pudding

1/2 C. sugar
3 T. pure cocoa
1/4 C. cornstarch
1/8 tsp. salt

2 3/4 C. whole milk
2 T. unsalted butter
1 tsp. GF pure vanilla

In a saucepan, on the stove, over medium heat, whisk sugar, cocoa, cornstarch and salt. Gradually whisk in milk. Keep whisking until mixture comes to a boil and is thickened. Remove from heat. Add vanilla and butter. Pour into custard cups and let cool. Can cover with plastic wrap on top cooked pudding if you do not want a pudding skin to form. Yield: 4 servings

Slovenian Wedding Cookies
Truly a "butter" ball

- 2/3 C. brown rice flour
- 3 T. potato starch
- 1 T. + 2 tsp. tapioca flour
- 1 tsp. xanthan gum
- 1/4 C. almond flour
- 2 C. unsalted butter, cut into slices
- 2 tsp. GF pure vanilla
- 1/2 C. powdered sugar + extra for double dusting of cookies
- 1/8 tsp. salt
- 1 C. nuts, ground, walnuts or pecans
- GF pure cooking spray

Preheat oven to 300°. Sift together brown rice flour, potato starch, tapioca flour and gum. Whisk in almond flour. Beat butter with an electric mixer and add powdered sugar, vanilla, water, and nuts until well mixed. Add flours to butter mixture and beat until well combined. Wrap dough in plastic wrap and chill overnight, at least 8 hours. Cover a cookie sheet with parchment paper. Spray the sheet with cooking spray. Place 1 inch balls, 1 inch apart on cookie sheet. Bake for 12 minutes. While still warm, sift powdered sugar on top of cookies. Cool and re-roll in powdered sugar so cookies are completely covered in sugar. Yield: 2 or more dozen

S'Mores

- 1/2 C. brown rice flour
- 2 1/2 T. potato starch
- 1 T. + 3/4 tsp. tapioca flour
- 1/4 tsp. xanthan gum
- 3 T. almond flour
- 3/4 C. GF graham crackers
- 1/2 C. light brown sugar, packed
- 1 C. unsalted butter
- 1 large beaten egg
- GF pure cooking spray

Topping:
- 3/4 C. semisweet chocolate
- 3/4 C. milk chocolate
- 2 T. whipping cream
- 1 C. miniature marshmallows
- 1/2 C. pecans or walnuts, chopped

Preheat oven to 350°. Sift together all dry ingredients except almond flour and cracker crumbs. Combine flour mixture, almond flour, cracker crumbs and brown sugar in a food processor. Pulse to mix. Add butter until mix becomes coarse. Add egg until just combined. Press dough evenly into the bottom of foil lined, greased, 9 x 13 pan. Bake 20 to 25 minutes. While crust is baking, prepare topping.

Topping: Chop 3/4 cup of semisweet chocolate and 1/4 cup of milk chocolate and microwave for 30 seconds. Stir and microwave at 30 second increments until melted. Set aside. As soon as crust comes out of oven, sprinkle remaining chocolate, marshmallows and pecans over crust and press down lightly with fingers. Drizzle melted chocolate over the top and return to oven. Bake until marshmallows puff up and lightly brown, 7 or 8 minutes. Cool in baking pan on a wire rack. Refrigerate until the topping is firm. Lift uncut cookies out of pan keeping foil on and cut into 20 bars.

Thumbprint Cookies

3 C. unsalted butter
1 C. sugar
1 tsp. GF pure vanilla
3 C. GF pastry flour see Two Flowers recipe
1/2 C. almond flour
1/2 C. finely ground nuts
1/4 tsp. salt
1 egg, beaten
1/2 C. sweetened coconut
Xanthan gum is included in Two Flowers recipe

Preheat oven to 325°. In a bowl, sift all dry ingredients except almond flour. Whisk in almond flour. In a separate bowl, combine butter and sugar and beat on high until fluffy. Add egg and beat until all is combined. Add flour and mix until incorporated. Chill 2 hours. Drop 1 inch balls onto a greased, parchment lined cookie sheet. Space them 2 inches apart. Make an indentation in the center, with your thumb moistened with water and fill with a spoonful of your favorite jam. Bake 12 minutes. Cool on wire racks. Yield: 30 or more cookies

White Chocolate Oatmeal Bars

Crust:
- 1 1/2 C. packed dark brown sugar
- 2 1/2 sticks butter
- 1 tsp. GF pure vanilla
- 3/4 C. brown rice flour
- 3/4 C. sweet rice flour
- 1/2 C. tapioca flour
- 1 T. cornstarch
- 1 tsp. xanthan gum
- 1 tsp. baking powder, see Two Flowers recipe
- 1/2 tsp. salt
- 2 C. GF oats

Filling:
- 12 oz. white chocolate chips
- 1 C. walnuts, chopped
- 2 C. butterscotch sauce
- 2 T. brown rice flour
- 2 T. sweet rice flour
- 1 tsp. cornstarch
- Butterscotch Sauce see Two Flowers recipe

Preheat oven to 350°. For the crust beat sugar, butter, vanilla together in a mixer. In another bowl, mix the rest of the dry ingredients together. Add oats to dry ingredients and add all dry ingredients to sugar and butter mix. In a greased 9 x 13 pan pat in 1/2 the mixture. Bake for 10 minutes. Remove from oven.

Filling: Sprinkle white chips over the cooked crust. Heat the homemade butterscotch sauce and stir in the flours and cornstarch. Drizzle this mixture over the chips. Crumble the remaining dough over the crust. Bake 25 more minutes until golden brown. Cool completely. Yield: 24 bars

Vegetables & Rice

Carrots in Almond Sauce

1 lb. carrots, peeled and cut into small sticks
1/2 C. green onions, bulbs and tops, sliced
1/4 C. unsalted butter
1 tsp. cornstarch
1/2 C. GF chicken broth, see Two Flowers recipe
1/2 tsp. fresh dill, minced
1/8 tsp. pepper
1/4 C. almonds, toasted

Cook carrots in a small amount of water so they steam. You do not want to boil them. Cook to a crisp-tender stage. Drain and set aside. In the same pan sauté onions in butter until soft. Dissolve cornstarch in broth stirring to remove any clumps and add to the onions. Add seasonings. Cook until it thickens. Add almonds and stir. Pour over warm carrots and toss. Yield: 4 to 6 servings

Corn Fritters

2 eggs, beaten
2 C. corn, fresh or frozen, thawed
1/4 tsp. sea salt
1 tsp. sugar
4 T. GF all purpose flour, see Two Flowers recipe
1 T. unsalted butter, melted
1/4 C. peanut oil for frying
Pure maple syrup

In a large bowl, beat eggs and mix in all other ingredients. Stir to combine but do not beat mixture. Heat oil in a skillet to 375°. Drop 1 tablespoon batter per fritter into oil and fry for 3 to 4 minutes until golden. Can serve with PURE maple syrup. Yield: 4 servings

Creamed Spinach
Using fresh nutmeg really makes a difference in this dish

- 4 pkg. chopped frozen spinach, 10 oz. each or equivalent
- 4 T. unsalted butter, melted
- 2 red onions, chopped
- 1/4 tsp. nutmeg
- 1 T. sea salt
- 1/4 tsp. pepper
- 2 T. tapioca flour
- 2 C. cold whole milk
- 1 C. whipping cream
- 1 C. Parmesan cheese, grated
- 1 C. Swiss cheese, grated

Preheat oven to 400°. Place defrosted spinach in a strainer and press out all water. Sauté onions in butter until golden brown. Add all seasonings. Mix tapioca flour with 1/2 cup milk and whisk well. Add rest of milk and cream to onion mixture. Cook until hot. Add flour milk mixture to onion mixture and cook until the sauce thickens. Mix in spinach and cheeses. Put in a greased 9 x 13 pan and bake at 400° uncovered for 25 to 30 minutes. It will bubble a bit and be slightly brown on the edges. Serve warm. Yield: 8 servings

Diner Rings
Onion rings

- 1 C. GF all purpose flour, see Two Flowers recipe
- 1 C. white rice flour
- 1 T. chili powder
- 1 tsp. baking soda
- 1/4 tsp. garlic powder
- 1/4 tsp. sea salt
- 1/4 tsp. pepper
- 1 1/4 C. cold club soda
- 1 large Vidalia onion or other sweet yellow onion, peeled and separated into rings
- Canola oil for frying

Heat oil to 385°. Whisk flours together. Combine flours, chili powder, baking soda, garlic powder, salt and pepper in a bowl. Slowly add club soda and continue whisking until smooth. Dip the onion rings one at a time into batter. Fry at 385° for about a minute on each side until golden brown. Drain on paper towels and keep warm in a 200° oven as you fry remaining rings. Sprinkle with additional sea salt if desired. Yield will depend upon the size of onion and how many rings you cut.

Fruited Cornbread Stuffing

- 1 C. cornmeal
- 1 C. GF all purpose flour, see Two Flowers recipe
- 1 T. baking powder, see Two Flowers recipe
- 2 T. sugar
- 1/2 tsp. sea salt
- 1/8 tsp. ground pepper
- 2 eggs, beaten
- 1 C. milk

Stuffing:
- 1/4 C. canola oil
- 1/2 C. golden raisins
- 1/2 C. dried apricots, slivered
- 1/2 C. dried cranberries
- 1 C. dry red wine
- 1/4 C. unsalted butter
- 1 C. sweet yellow onion, chopped
- 1 garlic clove, minced
- 1/2 C. celery, diced
- 1/2 C. green apple, diced
- 1 T. dried sage
- 2 C. GF chicken broth, see Two Flowers recipe
- 1/4 C. parsley, chopped
- 1 C. almonds, slivered, toasted

Corn bread: Preheat oven to 400°. Grease an 8 inch square pan with butter. Stir together cornmeal, flour, sugar, baking powder and salt. Stir together eggs, milk and oil. Add the wet ingredients to the dry ingredients. Mix well. Pour into the prepared baking pan. Bake for 30 minutes. Use a toothpick to test the center of the bread to make sure it is baked. Cool. Cut the bread into cubes and let it dry overnight. To make the stuffing, soak the dried fruit in the red wine for 1 hour. Meanwhile, in a large skillet, melt the butter. Add onions and garlic. Sauté until soft. Add celery, apple and sage to the skillet. Sauté for a few minutes more. Strain the dried fruit and discard the wine. Add the chicken broth to the bread cubes. Add all the ingredients to the bread and mix well. Put stuffing into a greased 9 x 13 Pyrex and bake at 325° for 30 minutes. Crank up the oven to 375° for 30 minutes longer. Yield: 8 or more cups

Garlicky Gouda Potato Casserole
A non-cream based casserole

- 2 C. Gouda cheese, shredded
- 2 T. garlic cloves, crushed
- 4 tsp. fresh thyme, minced
- 2 T. unsalted butter
- 1/4 C. GF all purpose flour, see Two Flowers recipe
- 4 C. GF chicken broth, see Two Flowers recipe
- 2 bay leaves
- 4 lbs. Yukon gold potatoes, peeled and sliced
- 3/4 tsp. salt
- 1/4 tsp. pepper

Preheat oven to 400°. Peel potatoes and put them in cold water to prevent discoloration but do not slice them until right before assembling the casserole. Melt butter and whisk in flour. Gradually add chicken broth and bay leaves. Bring to a boil. Reduce heat and continue to cook until mixture thickens. Take out bay leaf and cover sauce to keep it warm. Slice the potatoes in the food processor and layer them, slightly overlapping, in a greased 9 x 13 baking casserole dish. Make at least 3 layers. Sprinkle salt and pepper and 1 1/2 cups of shredded cheese evenly over each layer. Pour over the layered potatoes with the warm sauce. Cover the top of the casserole with plastic wrap, then with foil. Make sure you completely cover the plastic wrap with the foil. Bake 45 minutes. Yes, you can bake with plastic wrap! Nothing will stick to it. Remove the plastic wrap and foil. Sprinkle with remaining cheese and allow the potatoes to brown. Let the potatoes cool for a few minutes for cheese and sauce to set before serving. You may substitute your favorite creamy cheese for the Gouda. Yield: 8 servings

Gorgonzola Polenta

- 1/3 C. Gorgonzola or blue cheese
- 1 1/2 C. whole milk
- 1 1/2 C. GF chicken broth, see Two Flowers recipe
- 1 C. cornmeal
- 1/4 C. heavy cream
- DO NOT ADD SALT

Bring chicken broth and whole milk to a boil. Whisk in cornmeal and simmer until thickened. Stir in Gorgonzola or blue cheese and heavy cream. You can substitute milk for cream, but cream does make it creamy! Yield: 4 servings

Hash Browns with Goat Cheese
Kara Koprowski

3 to 4 large Yukon Gold potatoes, peeled
1/2 cup sweet yellow onion, grated or finely chopped
2 large egg whites, well beaten
1/3 C. rice flour
1/2 C. fresh goat cheese, crumbled
1 tsp. salt
1 tsp. black pepper
1 to 2 T. fresh parsley or chives, chopped

Preheat oven to 200°. Grate potato in food processor or by hand using box grater. Rinse the potatoes in a colander until water runs clear. Squeeze dry with your hands and then continue to squeeze the potatoes in a clean kitchen towel. In a large bowl, combine eggs whites, rice flour, goat cheese, salt, pepper and herbs. Add grated potatoes and onions. Stir well. Heat 1 to 2 tablespoons canola oil in a large frying pan on medium heat. Oil will be hot enough to fry after a small amount of hash brown mixture is added to oil and it sizzles. Scoop 1/2 cup of the potato mixture into the oil and flatten with a spatula. Fry on one side until golden brown, approximately 3 minutes. Flip and fry the other side until golden brown. Remove from pan and drain on paper towels. You may keep warm in a 200° oven until you are done frying the remaining potatoes. Can sprinkle with additional salt if needed. For spicier hash browns you can add a few dashes of red pepper flakes to potato mixture. Yield 4 servings

Hash Brown Muffins
Not a real muffin but a potato side dish

6 eggs
2 oz. Greek yogurt
1/2 tsp. sea salt
1/4 tsp. black pepper
1/4 C. unsalted butter
1/4 C. chives, chopped
1/4 C. green onions, tops and bulbs, sliced
1/4 C. red and green pepper, diced
1 C. russet potatoes, shredded
1/2 C. cheddar cheese, shredded
1/2 C. spicy cheese of choice, shredded

Preheat oven to 350°. Mix the 2 cheeses together. Beat eggs with yogurt and seasoning. Stir in chives. Melt butter in a skillet and sauté peppers and onions. Add the shredded potatoes and cook them until they are brown. Remove from heat. Divide potatoes into 12 portions. Press potato mixture into the bottom of 12 muffin cups. Pat it up on the sides leaving an area in the center empty. Divide the cheese into the muffin cups. Top with the remaining potato mixture. Pour the egg/yogurt mixture slowly into each muffin. Bake at 350° for 20 to 25 minutes until browned. Cool slightly and pop each muffin out. Yield: 12 muffins

Lemony Spring Risotto

- 6 C. chicken broth, see Two Flowers recipe
- 4 T. unsalted butter, cut into slices
- 2 green onions, bulbs and tops, chopped
- 1 C. Arborio rice
- 1/2 tsp. sea salt
- 1/4 tsp. white pepper
- 1/2 C. sweet white wine
- 12 thin asparagus spears, steamed and still crisp
- 1 C. frozen peas, thawed and drained
- 1 tsp. lemon zest
- 2 T. fresh lemon juice
- 1 C. parsley, chopped
- 1/2 C. Parmesan cheese, grated

Bring the chicken broth to a boil. Turn off the heat. In another saucepan, sauté the onions in the butter. Cook until tender. Add rice to the butter and onions and cook for 3 minutes. Add wine and lemon juice to mix and cook until liquid is absorbed. Add 1/2 cup of the broth to mix and continue cooking until the broth is gone. Keep adding the chicken broth to rice and stir with a wooden spoon a 1/2 cup at a time. All together it should take about 15 minutes to cook and stir the rice. The rice will be creamy when it is done. Stir in peas and asparagus. The whole process will take about 20 minutes. Sprinkle with lemon zest and cheese. Yield: 8 side dish servings

Noodle Kugel
Slovenian noodles

- 8 oz. GF medium wide noodles, see Two Flowers recipe
- 1 1/2 C. cottage cheese
- 1 C. sour cream
- 3 egg yolks
- 1 C. crushed pineapple, drained
- 1/4 C. sugar
- 1/2 C. golden raisins
- 2 T. unsalted butter, cut into small dots
- 1/2 C. GF bread crumbs
- 1 tsp. cinnamon

Preheat oven to 350°. Cook noodles and drain. Squeeze out the pineapple. Combine the cottage cheese, raisins, and pineapple. Mix into the noodles. Butter an 8 x 8 baking dish and sprinkle 1/4 cup of the bread crumbs on the bottom of the pan. Pour in the noodle mixture. Combine the egg yolks, sour cream, cinnamon and sugar and pour over the noodle mixture. Top with butter and the remaining 1/4 cup of crumbs. Bake at 350° covered for 25 to 30 minutes. Yield: 6 servings

Oven-Baked Brown Rice
Foolproof

1 1/2 C. brown rice, not instant
2 1/3 C. GF chicken broth, see Two Flowers recipe
2 tsp. unsalted butter
1/2 tsp. sea salt
1/8 tsp. pepper
1/2 C. parsley, chopped

You may substitute water or vegetable broth to make this vegetarian.

Preheat oven to 375°. Coat the bottom of an 8 inch square pan with butter. Spread rice evenly on the bottom of pan. Bring broth and butter to a boil in a saucepan on the stove. Add salt and pepper. Pour the hot liquid over the rice. Cover with a layer of plastic wrap and then foil on top of the plastic wrap, sealing the edges. Bake for 1 hour. Uncover and fluff with a fork. Add the parsley for color. Yield: 4 cups

Oven-Fried French Fries

5 large russet potatoes, unpeeled
1/4 C. olive oil
1/2 C. Parmesan cheese, grated
1/2 tsp. sea salt
1/4 tsp. black pepper

Scrub potatoes well and remove any tough or rough spots. Cut potatoes into wedges and put into a pot of cold water. Bring to a boil. Turn down heat and cook approximately 8 minutes until they are about three quarters of the way cooked. It is best to test on one wedge. Everything but the center of the potato will be cooked and slightly soft. Drain well. Toss wedges with oil, salt and pepper and bake at 400° until lightly browned. Sprinkle with Parmesan cheese and bake a few more minutes until cheese melts. Yield: about 3 to 5 servings. The amount will depend on upon the size of the potato. Can omit cheese if desired.

Oven-Roasted Brussels Sprouts

1 1/2 lbs. fresh Brussels sprouts, halved and tough outer leaves trimmed
3/4 tsp. coarse sea salt
1/4 tsp. pepper
4 T. olive oil
Garnish: optional but so good
1/2 C. walnuts, chopped
4 slices bacon, cooked

Preheat oven to 375°. Lightly grease a cookie sheet with 2 tablespoons of oil. Wash sprouts and dry on a paper towel. Place on the prepared pan and bake for 20 minutes. Check to make sure the sprouts are soft in the middle before taking them out. Can stir half way through baking time. Garnish with cooked bacon and walnuts. Yield: 4 servings

Polish Potato Pancakes

6 starchy baking potatoes, Yukon gold are a good choice
1 tsp. lemon juice
1/2 C. sweet onion, chopped
3 T. white rice flour
1 T. potato starch
3 eggs, beaten
1/4 tsp. nutmeg
1/4 tsp. sea salt
1/8 tsp. black pepper
Canola oil for frying
Applesauce, see Two Flowers recipe
Sour cream

Preheat 200°. Grate raw potatoes and onion together. A food processor works well if you do not want to grate by hand. There is no need to peel potatoes. Add lemon juice to potatoes to keep them from turning black. Squeeze out excess liquid from the onion/potato mixture. Do this as quickly as possible. A coffee filter placed in a fine strainer works well to help squeeze out liquid. When mixture is as dry as possible, add flour, starch and seasonings. Mix in eggs. In a frying pan, cover bottom with 1/4 inch oil and heat over medium heat. Use 1/8 measuring cup to make a 3 inch pancake. Turn once after a few minutes or when bottom is golden brown. Cook an additional 3 to 5 minutes. Drain on paper towels. You can keep pancakes warm in a 200° oven while frying remaining pancakes. Sprinkle with salt. If you are serving them later you can re-crisp in a 400° oven for a few minutes. Serve with applesauce and sour cream. Yield: about 12 pancakes

Quinoa Corn Cakes with Black Bean Salsa

1/2 C. quinoa, rinsed and drained
1/2 C. water
1 egg
1/2 C. GF chicken broth, see Two Flowers recipe
1/2 C. fresh or frozen corn, thawed
1/2 C. sweet onion, chopped
1/4 C. mozzarella cheese, shredded
1/4 C. GF all purpose flour, see Two Flowers recipe
2 T. buttermilk or sour cream
1/4 tsp. salt
1/8 tsp. pepper
Canola oil for frying

Salsa:
2 C. dried black beans, cooked
1 1/2 C. diced plum tomatoes, seeds discarded
1 small fresh jalapeno pepper, finely chopped, seeds and membrane removed
1/4 C. cilantro, chopped
1/4 C. green, red or yellow pepper, finely chopped, use all three
2 T. red wine vinegar
1 T. olive oil
Fresh lime juice from 2 lime wedges
Salt and pepper to taste
Sour cream for garnish

See Two Flowers recipe for cooking dried beans. Use gloves when chopping jalapeno peppers. Preheat oven to 200°. Add quinoa to broth and water and simmer on low heat for 15 minutes covered. Stir with a fork. Combine cooked quinoa with all other ingredients except oil until just combined. On a griddle or in a skillet, cover bottom of pan with oil and heat over medium heat. Use 1/4 cup mounds and flatten mounds with a fork. Turn once after 3 to 4 minutes or when bottom is golden brown. Cook an additional 2 to 3 minutes. Drain on paper towels. Can keep cakes warm in a 200° oven while frying remaining cakes. Sprinkle with salt. Combine salsa ingredients in a bowl and serve on top of the cakes. Also good with a dollop of sour cream on top of cakes. Yield: 4 to 6 servings

Red Cabbage and Apples
Kara Koprowski

- 1/4 C. unsalted butter
- 2 medium sized cooking apples sliced with skins on or can remove skins
- 1 medium sweet yellow onion, sliced
- 1 medium head red cabbage, core removed and thinly sliced
- 1/2 C. apple cider vinegar or apple juice
- 1/2 C. red wine vinegar
- 1 tsp. salt
- 1 tsp. pepper

Combine all ingredients in large saucepan and bring to a boil. Cover and simmer for 20 minutes. Add sliced apples. Cover and cook another 20 minutes until all ingredients are softened. Make sure cabbage and apples still retain their shape. You do not want to turn this to mush. Yield: 6 to 8 servings

Rice Stuffing
Makes a great side dish too

- 1/4 C. unsalted butter
- 1/4 C. celery, chopped
- 1 C. fresh parsley, chopped
- 1/4 C. onion, minced
- 1 tsp. sea salt
- 1/8 tsp. black pepper
- 1/4 tsp. tarragon
- 1/4 tsp. marjoram
- 1/4 tsp. sage
- 4 C. GF chicken broth, see Two Flowers recipe
- 3 C. cooked wild rice, do not use seasoning mix if using a box item

Optional Additions:
- 1 C. dried cranberries
- 1 C. dried apricots, slivered
- 1 C. walnuts or pecans, chopped

In a skillet melt butter. Sauté celery and onion. Cook until tender. Add seasonings and parsley. Combine with cooked rice. May be made 1 to 2 days ahead as long as you refrigerate the mix. Can also toast nuts if using in a dry skillet before adding them to cooked rice. Yield: 4 1/2 cups plus any additions. Yield: 6 to 8 cups depending upon your additions.

Sausage and Cornbread Stuffing

- Baked GF cornbread, see Two Flowers recipe
- 1 lb. GF sausage, crumbled
- 1 C. unsalted butter
- 2 C. celery, diced
- 2 C. onions, chopped
- 2 large eggs, beaten
- 1 1/2 T. GF poultry seasoning, see Two Flowers recipe
- 1 tsp. sea salt
- 1 tsp. black pepper
- 2 C. GF chicken broth, see Two Flowers recipe

Preheat oven to 350°. Prepare corn bread from Two Flowers recipe in the bread category. Cook crumbled sausage in a large pan until browned and cooked through, approximately 5 to 7 minutes. Drain. Add 1/2 cup butter to pan. Add chopped onion and celery and cook over medium heat until soft. Melt 1/4 cup butter and add to eggs and seasonings. Mix well. Combine everything together with diced cornbread. Make sure it is not wet, just moist. Grease a rectangular or oval baking dish and pat mixture into baking dish. Cube 1/4 cup remaining butter and add cubes into top of dressing, pressing down into casserole. Pour 1/2 cup chicken broth over the top to keep it moist. Bake at 350° uncovered until lightly browned, about 30 minutes. Yield: 8 servings

Scalloped Potatoes

- 6 baking potatoes, peeled and sliced
- 1/4 C. onion, chopped
- 3 T. sweet rice flour
- 1/4 C. unsalted butter, cubed
- 1/2 tsp. sea salt
- 1/4 tsp. pepper
- 1 C. white cheddar cheese, shredded
- 2 C. whole milk
- 2 T. parsley, minced

Preheat oven to 350°. Grease a 9 x 13 pan. Layer 1/2 the potatoes in the baking pan and top with 1/2 of the onions and 1/2 the flour. Sprinkle salt and pepper on potatoes. Dot with butter and 1/2 the cheese. Reserve the rest of the cheese. Repeat with layers omitting the cheese. In a saucepan scald the milk and pour over the potato layers. Cover with foil and bake for 45 minutes at 350°. Remove the foil, sprinkle with the reserved cheese and bake for another 15 minutes. Sprinkle with parsley. Yield: 6 servings

Slovenian Plum Dumplings
This dumpling was my grandmother Sternen's recipe

1 1/2 lbs. mashed potatoes
2 large eggs, beaten
1 tsp. sea salt
2 C. GF all purpose flour, see Two Flowers recipe
1/2 tsp. xanthan gum
1/2 C. sugar

1 tsp. cinnamon
1/4 tsp. nutmeg
15 small fresh plums, pitted
1/4 C. unsalted butter
1/4 C. GF stale bread crumbs, toasted in the oven

Put mashed potatoes, eggs, and seasonings in a bowl. Add flour, gum and salt to make a dough. Mix cinnamon, nutmeg and sugar together and pack a spoonful inside each plum. Take a piece of dough and flatten with your hand to make a circle, enough to cover each plum all the way around. Use your fingers to form the dumpling after wrapping dough around the plum. After all the plums are wrapped in dough and formed, drop the dumplings into a pot of boiling water. Bring the water back to a boil and cook gently for 5 to 7 minutes. Reduce the heat and simmer for 15 minutes. Drain and drizzle with melted butter and sprinkle toasted GF bread crumbs on top. Yield: 15 dumplings.

Spaetzle Noodles

2 1/2 C. GF all purpose flour, see Two Flowers recipe
1/2 tsp. xanthan gum
6 eggs, beaten, room temperature
1/2 C. water

1/4 tsp. sea salt
1/4 tsp. pepper
2 T. parsley, finely chopped
4 C. GF chicken broth, see Two Flowers recipe
Melted butter for drizzling

Mix eggs, parsley, water, and seasoning together. Add flour and gum to mixture. Mix well to form a dough. Form small pieces of pasta by pressing dough through the wide cut side of a box grater or drop small pinches of dough off the side of a knife into boiling broth or water. Drizzle with butter and additional salt if desired. Yield: 6 to 8 servings

Spinach and Artichoke Risotto

2 T. olive oil
2 T. garlic, minced
4 C. frozen artichoke hearts, thawed
1 1/2 C. sweet white wine
2 C. red onion, diced
2 1/2 C. Arborio rice
8 C. GF chicken broth, heated, see Two Flowers recipe
10 C. fresh spinach
2 C. mixed cherry tomatoes. chopped, such as pear, grape
1 C. unsalted butter
1 C. Parmesan cheese, grated
1/4 tsp. sea salt
1/4 tsp. pepper

Sauté garlic in 1 tablespoon oil. Add artichokes and 1/2 cup of wine. Cook until tender. In another pan, heat the rest of the oil and sauté the onions until soft. Add rice and stir. Lightly brown the rice. Add remaining cup of wine and cook until all liquid is gone. Add 4 cups of broth to rice, stirring. Add 1/2 of the remaining broth and stir until rice absorbs the liquid. Add the final amount of broth and cook until liquid is absorbed. Add spinach and artichoke mixture. Stir well. Stir in tomatoes, butter and Parmesan. Season with salt and pepper and serve. Yield: 8 cups

Spinach and Ricotta Cheese Frittata
Kara Koprowski

4 eggs, beaten
1/2 tsp. pepper
Pinch salt
Pinch nutmeg
1 T. butter
3 white button mushrooms, sliced
2 C. fresh spinach, steamed and drained
3 T. ricotta cheese

Preheat oven to 325°. In medium size bowl, blend together eggs, pepper, salt and nutmeg. Heat a 6 inch non-stick, oven safe sauté pan over medium high heat. Add butter to pan and melt. Add mushrooms and sauté for 2 to 3 minutes until soft. Pour egg mixture into pan. Stir in spinach with a spatula. Sprinkle ricotta cheese on top. Cook for 1 to 2 minutes or until the egg mixture has started to set on the bottom. Place pan into oven and bake for 10 minutes until lightly browned and puffed up. Remove from oven with oven mitts and let cool for a minute. Handle will be warm. Use a spatula to slide frittata out of pan on to a plate and cut into wedges. Yield: Serves 2. Can double recipe for a 10 inch pan. Can substitute another cheese for ricotta such as Pacemen or goat cheese.

Streusel Topped Sweet Potatoes

8 medium sized sweet potatoes, not yams
6 T. unsalted butter, melted
1/2 tsp. nutmeg
1/4 tsp. cinnamon
1 T. GF pure vanilla
4 tsp. fresh lemon juice
4 eggs
1 1/2 C. light cream

Topping:
5 T. unsalted butter
1/2 C. GF all purpose flour, see Two Flowers recipe
1/2 C. packed light brown sugar
1/4 tsp. sea salt
1 C. pecans, chopped

Bake the sweet potatoes in a 400° oven for about 1 hour. You can also microwave them to save time. When soft and cooled, scoop out the pulp into a food processor bowl. Add the remaining ingredients and pulse until combined. Pour mixture into a greased 9 x 13 casserole dish. Use a dish that will end up fitting your potato amount because the size of the potato will change the size of the casserole dish. In a food processor, pulse topping ingredients until they are coarsely mixed. Spread the topping over the sweet potato mixture. Bake in a 350° oven, uncovered for 45 minutes. Let set for 10 minutes before serving. Yield: 6 to 8 servings

Sweet Potato Fries

Seasoning mix:
1 tsp. coarse sea salt
1/2 tsp. chili powder
1/2 tsp. garlic powder
1/2 tsp. cayenne pepper

Fry coating:
1 C. cornstarch
3/4 C. club soda, cold
4 medium sweet potatoes
Peanut oil for frying

Preheat oven to 200°. Do not cut the potatoes until you are ready to use them. Whisk the seasoning together and put into a bowl. Set aside. Make coating mix in a medium sized bowl. Heat the oil to 370°. Cut the potatoes into the desired lengths and about 1/4 inch thick. Dip the fries into the coating mix. Let drain on a rack before frying so that coating is not too thick. Work in small batches and fry a few potatoes at a time. Always bring the oil back to 370° before adding more potatoes so that they fry quickly and do not absorb the oil. A batch should fry in about 8 minutes. Once they are fried put them in a 200° oven to keep them warm. When finished frying, toss the warm fries in the seasoning mix and serve. Yield: 4 side portions

Sweet Potato Risotto

2 T. dry white wine
1/3 C. onion, chopped
1 garlic clove, minced
1 C. uncooked Arborio rice
1/2 C. sweet potatoes, cooked and mashed
4 C. GF chicken broth, see Two Flowers recipe
1/8 tsp. ground nutmeg
1/8 tsp. ground cinnamon
3 T. Parmesan cheese, grated plus additional for garnish
Fresh parsley

Heat wine to boiling. Add onion and garlic to wine and cook until onion is soft. Stir in rice. Cook until rice is golden brown. Stir in sweet potatoes and 1/2 cup chicken broth that has been heated. Cook uncovered, stirring until liquid is absorbed. Cook for another 20 minutes adding the rest of the chicken broth, small amounts at a time. Cook until rice is tender. Stir in the rest of the ingredients. Serve with snipped fresh parsley and additional Parmesan cheese. Yield: 4 servings

Sweet Rice Pilaf

1/4 C. pecan pieces or halves
2 T. olive oil
2 green onions, bulbs and tops, chopped
1 1/2 C. basmati or jasmine rice
1/4 C. dried cranberries or dried cherries
1/4 C. dried apricots, slivered
3 C. GF chicken broth, see Two Flowers recipe
Fresh parsley, chopped
1/4 tsp. salt
1/8 tsp. pepper

Toast pecans in a dry skillet until lightly browned. In a saucepan, sauté onions in olive oil for a few minutes. Add rice to the same pan and stir until golden brown. Add dried fruits. Add broth and bring mixture to a boil. Cover and simmer for 20 minutes. Make sure all the broth is absorbed and rice is soft. Add pecans, parsley, salt and pepper. Yield: About 4 cups

Vegetarian Fried Rice

- 2 T. canola oil
- 4 beaten eggs, room temperature
- 1/4 tsp. pepper
- 1/4 tsp. salt
- 2 C. green onions, bulbs and tops, sliced
- 1 C. carrots, shaved or shredded
- 1/4 C. red and/or green peppers, shredded
- 2 tsp. fresh ginger, grated and peeled, not powdered ginger
- 2 garlic cloves, minced
- 5 C. rice, cooked and chilled
- 1/4 C. GF soy sauce
- 1/2 tsp. salt
- 1 10 oz. pkg. frozen snow peas, thawed, or steamed fresh snow peas, cut into strips

Heat 2 teaspoons oil over medium heat in a wok or large frying pan. Add half the eggs, salt and pepper to make a thin egg pancake. Remove egg from pan and slice into strips. Clean pan. Heat remaining oil over medium high heat and add onions, carrots, peppers, ginger and garlic. Stir fry 1 minute. Add rest of beaten eggs, cold rice and peas. Stir fry 3 minutes more. Add cooked egg strips and soy sauce. Combine well. Yield 8 cups.

Vegetable Tart with Canadian Bacon

- 1 lb. GF frozen hash browns, thawed, Oreida Brand is GF
- 3 green onions, tops and bulbs, chopped
- 1 egg, beaten
- 1 tsp. fresh basil, chopped
- 1/4 tsp. sea salt
- Filling:
- 1 small zucchini, chopped
- 1 garlic clove, minced
- 3 slices GF Canadian bacon, chopped
- 2 C. fresh spinach, chopped, stems removed
- 1/4 C. tomatoes, chopped
- 1/4 tsp. salt
- 1/8 tsp. pepper
- 1 large egg
- 1/2 C. cheddar cheese, shredded
- Canola oil

Preheat oven to 350°. Combine potatoes, onions, egg, basil and salt. Press onto bottom of a pie plate or tart pan that has been greased lightly with 1 teaspoon canola oil. Bake at 350° for 30 minutes. The crust will be firm and lightly browned. In a large skillet, heat 1 teaspoon of canola oil. Add bacon, zucchini, and garlic. Cook for 2 minutes. Add spinach, tomatoes, salt and pepper and cook for 5 minutes more until liquid is absorbed. Remove from heat. Stir in beaten egg. Pour mixture into the potato crust. Sprinkle with cheese and bake for 25 minutes until set. Yield: 6 servings

NOTES

INDEX

Appetizers, Beverages & Dips

3 Cheese Fondue 13
Asparagus Fries 1
Bacon, Lettuce and Tomato Fritters 1
Baked Tortilla Chips 2
Banana Almond Smoothie 14
Beet Hummus 2
Blue Cheese Cheesecake 3
Cheese Straws 3
Cheesy Rice Balls 4
Chex Mix Munchies 4
Chicken Nuggets 5
Chili Cheese Squares 6
Chili Con Queso Dip 5
Citrus and Ginger Beer Cooler 15
Coconut Chicken Fingers 6
Crab Cakes 7
Crunchy Chicken Fingers 7
Energy Juice Drink 15
Greenish Smoothie 16
Hummus 8
Kale Chips 8
Microwave Popcorn 9
Mini Corn Dogs 9
Norwegian Salmon Spread 10
Seared Fingerling Potatoes with Gorgonzola Cream Dip 10
Spinach and Artichoke Dip 11
Spring Rolls 12
Sweet Potato Chips 12
White Bean Dip 13
White Hot Chocolate 16
Zucchini Fritters 14

Bread Products, Pancakes & Crusts

Almond Flour Thin Crust Pizza 17
Apple Almond Muffins 17
Banana Bread 18
Blueberry Muffins 18
Buckwheat Pancakes 19
Buttermilk Biscuits 19
Cheddar Sweet Sausage Muffins 20
Cheesy Bacon Quick Bread 20
Chocolate Marble Bread with Ganache 21
Cinnamon-Raisin Yeast Rolls .. 22
Clover Leaf Dinner Rolls 23
Cornbread 23
Cranberry-Nut Bread 24
Crispy Parmesan Shells 24
Frenchy Crepe Pancakes 25
Golden Waffles 25
Hash Brown Crust 26
Kalamata Olive Bread 26
Lemon Bread with Lemony Glaze 27
Pasta Dough 28
Pepper Jack Cheese Pancakes 29
Pie Crust 30
Pizz-a-ria Pizza Crust 30
Raspberry Cornmeal Muffins 31
Rice Crust for Quiche or Pies 31
Rosemary Focaccia Bread 32
Shortcake Biscuits 33
Southern Spoonbread 33

i

Sweet Italian Sausage Quick Bread 34
Sweet Potato Bread 34
Tea Bread 35
White Bread 36

Make Your Own Mixes & Pantry Staples

All Purpose Flour Mix 37
Almond Granola..................... 37
Baking Powder 38
Bisquick Baking Mix Substitute 38
Breading Choices................... 38
Brown Sugar 39
Cajun Seasoning.................... 39
Classic Dry Chili Mix 39
Crumble Topping for Pies, Muffins and Cobblers 40
Dry Meat Rub........................ 40
Herb de Provence................... 40
Hot Cocoa Mix 41
Magic Seasoning 41
Methods for Cooking Dried Beans................................ 42
Muffin Mix 42
Onion Soup Mix 43
Pancake Mix.......................... 43
Pastry Flour........................... 43
Poultry Seasoning 44
Self- Rising Cornmeal Mix 44
Self- Rising Flour................... 44
Taco Seasoning...................... 44
Terrific "Breading" 45

Satisfying Meals

Asian Spicy Shrimp Noodle Bowl 47
Baked Florentine Sole............ 48
Beef Stroganoff Revisited 49
Breakfast Bake 50
Bruschetta Chicken 51
Cantonese Style Stir Fry 52
Cheesy Crab Bake 53
Chicken Divan....................... 54
Chicken or Beef Enchiladas ... 54
Chicken Paprikash with Noodles.............................. 55
Chicken Stew with Dumplings 56
Creamy Scrambled Eggs 56
Crispy Chicken 57
Crock Pot Macaroni and Cheese................................ 57
Crustless Bacon and Broccoli Quiche................................ 58
Dutch Baby Breakfast Pancake 58
Fennel-Crusted Pork Loin with Roasted Vegetables and Pears 59
Flounder Piccata.................... 59
Greek Shrimp Risotto............ 60
Green Tea Poached Fish........ 60
Ham & Aspargus Rice Bake.... 61
Mac & Cheese........................ 62
Pad Thai................................ 63
Potato Crusted Quiche 64
Pretzel Chicken..................... 64
Quinoa Stuffed Peppers........ 65
Retro Pot Roast 66
Salmon with Ginger Soy Sauce................................. 67
Salmon, Roasted in the Oven with Tangerine Relish................................ 67
Sausage Breakfast Patties 68
Southwestern Lasagna 69

Spaghetti Squash "Noodles" with Sauteed Vegetable Sauce...... 70
Spinach Polenta Torte............ 71
Swedish Meatballs 72
Tilapia Tacos 73
Tortilla Bake 73
Vegetable Quiche Cups.......... 75
Vegetarian Chili, Oven Roasted 74
Veggie Burgers 75
White Autumn Vegetable Lasagna 76

Sauces & Dressings

1,000 Island Dressing............ 92
Alfredo Sauce....................... 77
Apple and Sage Sauce for Pork................................ 77
Apricot or Blackberry Glaze.. 77
Avocado Vinaigrette 78
B.B.Q. Sauce.......................... 79
Basic White Sauce................. 78
Basil Pesto 79
Berry Jam 79
Berry Salsa 80
Berry Sauce 80
Blue Cheese Dressing............ 80
Broccoli Cream Sauce............ 81
Butterscotch Sauce 81
Caramelized Pineapple........... 81
Chocolate Peanut Butter Sauce............................. 82
Chocolate Sauce 82
Citrus Herb Sauce.................. 82
Citrus Herb Stir Fry or Dipping Sauce 83
Coconut Curry Stir Fry Sauce............................. 83

Creamy Tomato Sauce............ 84
Cutting Board Salsa 84
Dill Sauce 85
Ginger Dressing 85
Hoisin Sauce 85
Hot Bacon Dressing 85
Ketchup 86
Marsala Mushroom Sauce...... 87
Mayonnaise......................... 87
Peanut Butter 88
Popsi's Favorite Applesauce.... 88
Ranch Dressing 88
Red Wine Vinaigrette............ 89
Roasted Tomato Sauce........... 89
Smashed Onion Jam.............. 90
Stir Fry Sauce 90
Sweet & Sour Sauce.............. 91
Sweet Chili Sauce 91
Sweet Marinade.................... 91
Tartar Sauce........................ 92
Tomato and Arugula Pesto 92
Tomato Pineapple Salsa......... 93
Tomato Sauce....................... 93
Turkey Gravy 94
Vegetable Herb Sauce........... 94
Vegetable Pasta Sauce 95
Watermelon Salsa................. 95
White Clam Sauce................. 96

Soups & Salads

ABC Salad - Apple, Broccoli Cranberry....................... 115
Asian Salad Wraps 116
Avocado Lemon Shrimp Salad 117
Avocado Salad..................... 118
Baked Potato Soup 97
Beefy Broth 97

iii

Black Bean Soup 98
Brie and Asparagus Soup 98
Brown Rice with Tomatoes and Basil Salad 118
Buckwheat Noodle Salad 119
Cellophane Noodle Salad with Shrimp and Chicken... 119
Cheesy Onion Soup 99
Chicken Noodle Soup 99
Chicken Stock 100
Chinese Chicken Salad..........120
Cold Asian Noodles 120
Cold Beet Salad 121
Corn and Chicken Chowder...100
Corn and Quinoa Soup 101
Cornbread Salad 121
Creamy Spinach, Mushroom and Wild Rice Soup...........102
Creamy, NO Cream, Cauliflower Soup................ 101
Egg Drop Soup 102
Farina Ball Soup...................103
Fresh Mushroom Soup 103
Fresh Tomato Broth 104
Fresh Tropical Fruit Salad with Lemon Banana Dressing...........................122
Mango Slaw 123
Nana's Potato Salad 123
Peachy Cold Soup 104
Quinoa Salad with Cherries and Cashews....................124
Red Lentil Soup 105
Rice and Asparagus Orange Salad 124
Roasted Red Pepper and Eggplant Bisque.................106
Roasted Warm Beet Salad....125
Shredded Vegetable Salad with Easy Vinaigrette Dressing...........................126

Shrimp and Spinach Soup.....107
Shrimp Bisque Velvet............108
Split Pea Soup Updated........109
Summertime Vegetable Soup 110
Tex Mex Stew.......................111
Tomato Cream Soup............. 112
Vegetable Broth 114
Very Vegetable Turkey Chili.. 113
White Bean Soup with Bacon............................... 114
Wilted Kale Salad 127

Sweet Tooth

Angel Food Cake 129
Apple Cookies 129
Baked Apples, Crust-less 130
Brownies from the Past 130
Carrot Cake 131
Cheesecake Made Crustless........................134
Chocolate Chippies................132
Chocolate Cookies.................132
Chocolate Frosting................133
Chocolate Oatmeal No-Bake Drops.............................135
Chocolate Peanut Butter Cheesecake....................135
Chocolate Pie Filling 136
Chocolate Pound Cake 136
Chrusciki..............................137
Cinnamon and Spice Caramel Popcorn.............138
Coconut Chocolate Balls........ 131
Cream Cheese Frosting.........138
Cream Puffs.........................139
Cut-Out Sugar Cookies.........140
Date Bars............................ 141
Donuts 142

Double Chocolate Truffles..... 141
Dream Bars........................... 142
Festive Fudge....................... 143
Flourless Chocolate Cake...... 145
Fresh Peach Cobbler............. 144
Fruity Macaroons 145
Granola Bar on the Go......... 146
Gumdrops............................ 146
Ice Cream in the Food Processor........................... 147
Lemon Angel Pie 147
Luscious Lemon Bars............. 148
Melt-in-Your Mouth Lemon Drops................................ 149
Minty Chocolate Loaf Cake...150
Nut and Honey Bars.............. 151
Oatmeal Raisin Cookies........ 152
Oatmeal Snack Cake............. 153
Peanut Butter Cookies 154
Peanut Butter Haystacks....... 154
Pie Crust 155
Pineapple Upside-Down Cake 156
Pistachio Dacquoise (Meringue)....................... 157
Polish Cream Cheese Cookies............................. 158
Polish Custard Cake.............. 159
Rice Pudding 160
S'Mores 162
Simply Chocolate Pudding.....160
Slovenian Wedding Cookies... 161
Thumbprint Cookies.............. 163
White Chocolate Oatmeal Bars................................... 164

Vegetables & Sides

Carrots in Almond Sauce....... 165
Corn Fritters......................... 165
Creamed Spinach 166
Diner Rings 166
Fruited Cornbread Stuffing .. 167
Garlicky Gouda Potato Casserole 168
Gorgonzola Polenta...............168
Hash Brown Muffins 170
Hash Browns with Goat Cheese.............................. 169
Lemony Spring Risotto 171
Noodle Kugel....................... 171
Oven-Baked Brown Rice....... 172
Oven-Fried French Fries....... 172
Oven-Roasted Brussels Sprouts............................. 173
Polish Potato Pancakes 173
Quinoa Corn Cakes with Black Bean Salsa................ 174
Red Cabbage and Apples...... 175
Rice Stuffing........................ 175
Sausage and Cornbread Stuffing 176
Scalloped Potatoes 176
Slovenian Plum Dumplings 177
Spaetzle Noodles 177
Spinach and Artichoke Risotto 178
Spinach and Ricotta Cheese Frittata 178
Streusel Topped Sweet Potatoes............................ 179
Sweet Potato Fries................ 179
Sweet Potato Risotto............ 180
Sweet Rice Pilaf.................... 180
Vegetable Tart with Canadian Bacon.................. 181
Vegetarian Fried Rice........... 181

Two Flowers Food Company

How to purchase the Two Flowers Cookbook, Cooking Gluten Free; Healthy Recipes for Everyone

By Mail: $20.00 includes postage (cash, check or money order only; no credit cards at this time)

Payable to:

Two Flowers Food Company
302 North Main Street
Chagrin Falls, Ohio 44022

Please include your name, full mailing address and email so a confirmation can be sent to you.

Books are available at Trifles Catering, $17.00 each (cash, check or money order only; no credit cards at this time)

8284 East Washington Street
Chagrin Falls, Ohio 44023
440.247.8595

The eBook is available at amazon.com and barnesandnoble.com for $9.99.

For more information, visit our website at:

www.twoflowersfoodcompany.com

For the most up to date information, "Like" us on Facebook at Two Flowers Food Company.

Want more information? We would love to hear from you. Email us at: twoflowersfoodcompany@yahoo.com.

Happy, healthy eating!